UNTIL THE KING COMES

Sermons for Pentecost (Last Third)
Cycle C Gospel Texts
BY THEODORE F. SCHNEIDER

D1402358

C.S.S Publishing Co., Inc.
Lima, Ohio

Copyright © 1991 by
The C.S.S. Publishing Company, Inc.
Lima, Ohio

Library of Congress Cataloging-in-Publication Data

Schneider, Theodore F., 1934-
    Until the king comes : sermons for Pentecost (last third) : cycle C Gospel texts / by Theodore F. Schneider.
        p.   cm.
    Includes biographical references.
    ISBN 1-55673-316-X
    1. Pentecost season — Sermons.   2. Lutheran Church — Sermons.
3. Sermons, American.   I. Title
BV4300.5.S364   1991
252'.6 — dc20   91-4094
                                                                          CIP

9137 / ISBN 1-55673-316-X   PRINTED IN U.S.A.

To
Elisa Anne
and
Timothy Allen

Lo, children are a heritage from the Lord, a reward from Him.

—Psalm 127:3

Table Of Contents

All texts in this book are from the series for Lesson One, Common Lectionary. Lutheran and Roman Catholic designations indicate days comparable to Sundays on which Common Lectionary Propers are used.

Preface

What to do in the meantime? We have all been there! An appointment has been kept and there is some time until the next . . . too much time, it seems . . . just to wait, doing nothing. Yet the time is hardly enough to tend anything else. What does one do in the meantime?

From the beginning the church has lived in the meanwhile of time. Throughout the New Testament there is an urgency defined by a single word: "until."

Jesus was expected to return. The expectation is introduced in the gospels and is affirmed by the angels in the first chapter of the Acts of the Apostles. In the early epistles of Paul, we watch and listen as the early church takes a longer view of Christ's return. According to the latest of the epistles, 2 Peter, the delay in Christ's return is an act of God's intentional mercy.

Not only has the history of the church been lived in the "meanwhile" from the beginning, but that "meanwhile" has been of an unknown length.

Therefore, there has been from the beginning the urgent need for the Faithful of God to be ready at all times so that the Church can be ready "whenever." That Christ was coming on that great "day of the Lord" was certain in Jesus' teachings and the church's expectation. The issue has never been "if." It has always been "when."

Twenty centuries later, it remains the same. We are still living in the "meanwhile." God's purposes are yet being worked and history is moving to God's just conclusions. We have God's promise and upon that promise we are called to build our lives and carry out our baptized priesthood. As we tell the story of God's work for our salvation and of our role as ministers of this gospel, we come each year to the close of the church year. Each year we come to the story's conclusion and to these end time expectations. The church is always expecting Christ's coming, working faithfully as we wait, until the king comes.

This book of 13 sermons begins with the last half of the Pentecost Season, Series C. Already there is on the horizon "the beginning of the end." The coming of salvation into our lives (the 10 lepers and Zacchaeus) is matched with increasingly urgent emphases upon our response to God's grace. Steadfastness, trust, and faithfulness become recurring themes, often appearing in familiar parables ("the Unrighteous Judge," "the Pharisee and the Publican," and "the Parable of the Talents"), until the final closing Sunday's theme is announced and celebrated. Christ is the king in heaven and on earth.[1]

Thus this book's title and its theme: *Until The King Comes.*

Theodore F. Schneider

---

1. If the emphasis upon the "last things" appears to be somewhat unsteady as the year closes and the lessons unfold for us, the preacher/reader is reminded that this is an "elastic" part of the church's year, depending upon the date of Easter. Often one does not move so deeply into the late Pentecost Sundays before the theme of "Christ the King" bursts upon us. It remains for the preacher, then, to develop for his or her congregation this developing sense of urgency as these late Pentecost lessons appear.

Acknowledgments

We ought to make an effort to act on our first thoughts and let our unspoken gratitude find expression. Then there will be more sunshine in the world, and more power to work for what is good.

Memories of Childhood and Youth
Albert Schweitzer

There have been those who, from the beginning, have entered wholeheartedly into this enterprise with me. Perhaps it all began decades ago with the steady and at times urgent encouragement of a longtime parishioner and friend, Dr. Samuel Doughty, an engineer and college professor by vocation and a solid churchman by conviction, who urged that a young pastor (at that time!) give himself to the discipline of writing. More recently, there has been the active encouragement of my former seminary classmate and continuing colleague and friend, The Rev. Dr. Frank H. Seilhamer.

In the preparation of this manuscript, I am indebted to so many. There have been the patience and the support of the people and staff of Saint Luke Lutheran Church, who gave time, space, and caring support to the task. Mrs. Betty Fulton, Executive Secretary to the Senior Pastor, arranged and protected huge blocks of undisturbed time in a busy schedule, allowing me to plan, meditate and write.

Mr. Jeffrey R. Pannebaker, our Director of Music Ministry not only read manuscripts, but researched numerous details, quotes and items of specific history. His sound theological insights and appreciation for the liturgy and the church year brought forth significant enhancements to early drafts of the manuscript. Mr. Kirk Howard Betts, one of our key parish leaders, an astute listener and critic of preaching week by week, — and a friend — brought skills as an attorney to the detailed correctness of both text and footnotes, suggested and encouraged significant clarifications, and added over and again the suggestions of one who needs make no apologies as a theologian. Mrs. Donna Ward Smith, a journalist, graciously brought her professional skill and her remarkable knowledge of the Scriptures to the reading and editing of early versions of each of the sermons. My clergy colleagues, The Rev. Dr. Harold G. Deal and The Rev. Mark A. Rossman have steadily given their encouragement and have taken manuscripts to read.

Finally, I must give special gratitude to my wife, Doris Lee. Gifted with a mind for the organization of work and materials, she gave long hours, sometimes against deadlines, in skilled editing, in gathering together the notes and comments of all who entered with us into the process of editorial refinement, and in the preparation of the final printouts for the publisher. My love and gratitude abound all the more.

For all of these, and to countless others who shared in this enterprise, I herewith sing a loud *Te Deum*.

Theodore F. Schneider

To Be Sure . . .

I am always impressed with the litany-like phrases Martin Luther uses in *The Small Catechism* as petition by petition he explains the Lord's Prayer:

> *To be sure, God's name is holy itself . . .*
> *To be sure, the kingdom of God comes of itself, without our prayers . . .*
> *To be sure, the good and gracious will of God is done without our prayer . . .*
> *To be sure, God provides daily bread, even to the wicked, without our prayer . . .*[1]

To be sure, to be sure, to be sure! God's gifts come to us despite our unfaithfulness and often without our prayers. Paul quotes an ancient Christian hymn in his second letter to Timothy: "If we are faithless, he remains faithful — for he cannot deny himself (2 Timothy 2:13)." Our faithlessness and ingratitude cannot make of God something that he is not.[2] To sure!

All of which brings us to the heart of today's gospel. Rudolph Bultmann is quite correct when he notes that the emphasis of Luke's story is not the miracle of 10 lepers cleansed, but rather the contrast of gratitude and ingratitude depicted on the same dramatic canvas.[3]

Luke draws the contrast all the more boldly when he notes that the man returning to give thanks was a Samaritan, a "foreigner." Always the master storyteller among the four evangelists, Luke, having already given us the story of the "Good Samaritan," now gives us the story of the "Thankful Samaritan."

11

Twice An Outsider

The "Thankful Samaritan" in today's gospel is "twice an outsider."

It was enough that he was a Samaritan, and therefore a "foreigner." There was open hostility among Jews and Samaritans in Jesus' day. Enmity had been brewing for centuries, and especially since the return of the exiles from Babylon in the sixth century B.C.E.[4] Though it may be that by Jesus' day few remembered the stories of its origin, the hostility was mutally shared.

Believed by tradition to be the remnant of the lost tribes of Israel which disappeared after the fall of Samaria to Sargon II of Assyria in 722 B.C.E., the Samaritans had retained many of the traditions of their Hebrew heritage, including their version of the Pentateuch (the Torah) and festivals such as Passover. In 586 B.C.E. the Southern Kingdom, Judah, fell to the Babylonians and many of its leaders and people were carried into exile.

Upon the return of the exiles from Babylon in 538 B.C.E., the Samaritans offered their help in rebuilding the temple in Jerusalem, a generous gesture that turned their back upon the loyalties of the earlier traditions of the Northern Kingdom and the ancient patriarchal tradition for worship at Shechem, the valley between Mount Gerizim and Mount Ebal. Their offer was refused! Instantly there was hostility. The Samaritans countered by building their own rival temple on Gerizim, and by creating troublesome rumors about the exiles within the court of Cyrus, the Persian king. Though this Samaritan temple was destroyed by John Hyracnus in 128 B.C.E.[5], the rivalry over these two sites raged on into Jesus' day.

To be sure, and for all these reasons, the Samaritan was an outsider to the covenant and its promises by his choice and by the prejudice against him.

And, he was a leper! The law of the Pentateuch, both Samaritan and Hebrew versions, made him an "outsider" still another time.

"He is unclean; he shall dwell alone in a habitation outside the camp (Leviticus 14:46b)." To be "unclean" was to be unworthy of God and unfit for human companionship. Rabbis considered a leper to be as good as dead. Suggesting both ritual defilement and the judgment of God, lepers were "cleansed," not "healed." Priestly observation and verification were required before one was readmitted into the community. Clearly, to be healed meant the intervention of God.[6] It is no surprise, then, that the man, "when he saw that he was healed, turned back, praising God with a loud voice, and he fell at Jesus' feet, giving him thanks. (Luke 17:15-16)."

To be sure, the Samaritans was twice an outsider, and yet he was a recipient of God's grace. Outside the covenant, he would not be expected to understand and affirm God's hand in his healing. The contrast of gratitude and ingratitude is depicted clearly on one dramatic canvas.[7]

The Faithfulness Of God

Equally drawn for us is the faithfulness of God, though we may well overlook the text's other important insights as we fix ourselves upon the question of ingratitude. "Where are the other nine?" becomes for virtually all of us the focus of the entire text. Yet, much more is here that is of prime importance. For example:

1. The 10 lepers were not healed ("cleansed!") while in the presence of Jesus. It appears they left his presence unhealed and unaided. They were healed as they began the journey to show themselves to the priests, as the law required. It would appear that all 10 lepers were healed as they responded in obedience — trusting Jesus' words. "And as they went they were healed." Obedience has often been a cornerstone of Jesus' miracles.

2. We depend on Jesus' words to know that all 10 were cleansed ("Were not 10 cleansed? Where are the other nine?"). Only one returned to verify the miracle.

13

3. There is no evidence that God took back his healing from the "ungrateful nine." Ungrateful though they appear, they are allowed to keep the gift. Again we hear the words of 2 Timothy 2:11: "If we are faithless, he remains faithful, for he cannot deny himself."

4. The grateful man was a Samaritan! Be we leper or foreigner, no one is outside the reach and the concern of God's grace.

The breadth and depth of God's faithfulness to us are important parts of today's gospel. They are the fulcrum over which gratitude and ingratitude are balanced in this story and in our lives. God's faithfulness embraces the grateful and the ungrateful.

The inclusiveness of God's grace is not unique to the New Testament. For example, we have in 2 Kings 5:14-17 the story of Naaman, the commander of the army of the king of Syria. He was a leper who came to Elisha. He was healed as he washed himself, obediently, in the river Jordan. He, too, an outsider and a leper, returned to Elisha giving praise to God. In the Book of Ruth we find the grace of God extended to the faithful Moabite, Ruth. And, of course, there is the whole book of Jonah! In Isaiah 40:5a the inclusive purposes of God are made forcefully: "And all flesh shall see it together."

The prophet Joel would say it. Peter would preach it and Paul would write it: "Everyone who calls upon the name of the Lord will be saved." "Truly, I perceive that God shows no partiality," says Peter. Clearly, this is what this gospel proclaims: "And as he entered a village, he was met by 10 lepers, who stood at a distance and lifted up their voices and said, 'Jesus, Master, have mercy on us. (Luke 17:12-13)."

To be sure! Though we are faithless, God remains faithful, even patient and hopeful, for he cannot deny himself. He is the waiting father in the parable misnamed for the prodigal son.[8] The gifts God gives us are real. They become fully ours to use in our freedom. That is for us both the good news and the bad. It is good news because of God's gracious faithfulness. It becomes bad news when we turn these gifts to our own selfish uses as if we were the "ungrateful nine."

14

The Gifts God Gives

To be sure! God gives us seven days a week whether we care enough to return to give praise and thanks on the Sabbath. He created the Sabbath for us, not us for the Sabbath, providing us rest from the rigors of a daily routine and time to remember, and to be grateful for, all he has done for our salvation.

To be sure! He gives us food, raiment, family, friends and all we need in this daily life whether we are grateful enough to share with those who have less — bringing his grace to others.

To be sure! He has redeemed us, lost and condemned creatures who in our alienation are as foreigners, and in our sinfulness are as lepers. He has done so not with silver and gold, as Luther writes, but with the precious body and blood of his Son, our Lord Jesus Christ. And he has done it whether we care enough to thank him, praise him, or share his gifts with others, telling the good news of his love to those who stare into their own death with fear — and with numbed hopelessness!

To be sure! Nine lepers went careening on through life, claiming the gifts and celebrating their healing, believing they had everything. Many of us, in our own ways, join them! And ungracious though we are, God does not rescind his gifts.

Nonetheless, there is wondering sadness in Jesus' voice: "Were not 10 cleansed? Where are the other nine? Was no one found to return and give praise to God except this foreigner?" And he said to him, "Rise and go your way; your faith has made you well." One could almost weep with the Christ. Only one knew the joy and fullness of living life in gratitude. All but one missed the hugest of the miracles in today's story: "Get up and be on your way; your faith has brought you salvation."[9] All 10 were healed of leprosy. One was given still more. Just one heard Jesus' words about a new understanding of faith and of wholeness.

15

Still we take God's gifts and run! Over and again we claim the gifts and yet are absent from his house on the Sabbath, grudging and delinquent in our stewardship, and silent in our witness to him who heals us.

We take his gifts and run. But he gives them all the same. Though we are faithless, God remains faithful, for he cannot deny himself. It is God's nature to be faithful. Would, too, that it were ours.

We are alienated. We are the outsiders. We are the repeatedly unsure and the ungrateful. Again, Luther writes in *The Small Catechism:* "To be sure, God provides daily bread, even to the wicked, without our prayer, but we pray in this petition that God may make us aware of his gifts, and enable us to receive [them] . . . with thanksgiving."

Amen.

---

1. Martin Luther, "The Small Catechism," *The Book of Concord,* Theodore G. Tappert, Translator and Editor, (Philadelphia, Fortress Press, 1959), pp. 346-347.

2. Paul J. Achtemeier, *Proclamation 3,* Pentecost 3, Series C, (Philadelphia, Fortress Press, 1986), p. 19.

3. Joseph A. Fitzmyer, S.J., *The Gospel According to Saint Luke X-XXIV,* The Anchor Bible, Vol. 28A, (Garden City, N.Y., Doubleday and Company, Inc., 1985), p. 1149.

4. B.C.E. is now the preferred designation for dates previously coded as B.C. It is not preferential to a specific religious tradition. "Before Christ" becomes "Before the Contemporary Era" or "Before the Common Era."

5. Wilbers F. Howard, *The Interpreter's Bible,* Vol. 8, (New York, Abingdon Press, 1952), p. 526.

6. Paul J. Achtemeier, *op. cit.,* p. 20. Dr. Achtemeier provides a rather full discussion of this whole matter of the plight of the leper, socially and spiritually.

7. Joseph A. Fitzmyer, *op. cit.,* p. 1149.

8. Helmut Thielicke, *The Waiting Father*, John W. Doberstien, Translator, (New York, Harper and Row, Publishers, 1959), p. 29.

9. Joseph A. Fitzmyer, *op. cit.* p. 1148. This insightful translation comes much closer to understanding biblical healing as something more than being "without disease." It has to do with "shalom," which is to say, "Being with us as God wills." Only then are things "well" and at "peace."

What Will He Find . . . When He Comes?

Every pastor has been touched and troubled when there have been those in the congregation who suddenly have faced unemployment. Like an ambush from two sides, unemployment attacks us with the fear of financial insecurity on the one side and the loss of self-esteem on the other. Job searching can deepen both. In just such a moment I encountered Brian. He is a competent and creative person whose skills and personality cannot be long overlooked. "It will work out, Brian," I said. "God does provide." "I hope so!" he replied. From the inflection of his voice, I knew he did not "expect" so.

One is reminded of Lucy's encouragement to Charlie Brown in one of the *Peanuts* cartoons. "Look at it this way, Charlie Brown," she consoles. "These are your bitter days. These are the days of your hardship and struggle . . ." The next frame goes on: ". . . but if you just hold your head up high and keep on fighting, you'll triumph!" "Gee, do you really think so, Lucy?" Charlie asks. As she walks away Lucy says: "Frankly, no!"[1]

Hope is like that. We speak of it more often than we believe in it. Hope is not a strong word for us. It has more to do with "wishing" than "expecting." It has the sound of resignation, an inability to bring about, influence, or even believe that a desired event or goal might ever come to be. "Well, I hope so" has in its whimsical sound the same negation of the words that we hear in the sarcastic "Sure it will!" or "Well, I guess!" Hope, as we understand it, is not a word of excitement and expectation. It speaks of resignation and help-lessness. "Well, I hope so . . ."

How then can we understand the New Testament's strong use of the word? Repeatedly Paul writes about hope. To the Thessalonians he writes of the armor of God, including the "hope of salvation" as a helmet. To the Colossians he writes of the "hope laid up in heaven," and of the "hope of glory." Peter writes in his first letter that "we have been born anew to a living hope through the resurrection of Jesus Christ from the dead, and to an inheritance which is imperishable, unde-filed, and unfading, held in heaven for you."

Given our understanding of the word, shivers run up our spines as we think about it. "Is that all we have?" we want to shout. "Is 'hope' all we have after all? Just . . . hope?"

A Hope That Does Not Disappoint Us

How differently the Bible uses our word. Rather than resig-nation, the word bristles with excitement and expectation. It is for the writers of both the Old and New Testaments a strong word filled with encouragement. Consider Paul's words to the Christians at Rome:

> *We rejoice in our sufferings, knowing that suffering produces endurance and endurance produces character, and character produces hope, and hope does not disap-point us, because God's love has been poured into our hearts through the Holy Spirit which has been given us. (Romans 5:2-5).*

"Hope does not disappoint us!" Perhaps so, but our ex-perience of the word often has been otherwise. How can this be so?

The test is: "Upon what or whom is our hope based?" If our hope rests in "good luck" or an unexpected turn of the game late in the fourth quarter, then hope is likely to disappoint us. On the other hand, if our hope is based upon the integrity of God and his promises, built upon the gifts of the Holy Spirit, then the meaning and experience of hope is a different matter altogether.

It's more than a word game. A lively and excited hope is a necessary ingredient in the Christian life. Similarly, an understanding of the role hope plays is pivotal if we are to comprehend what Jesus would have us learn from his parable about the widow and the uncaring judge.

Hope has always been crucial to the church's faithful discipleship and the stewardship of the gospel, just as it has always been with God's chosen people of Old Testament times. Instantly we understand why when we read the words of 1 Samuel 3: "The word of the Lord was rare in those days: there was no frequent vision." This speaks neither of the eyesight nor of the spiritual sincerity of the people, but of their inability to experience the presence of God, the source of hope in their lives. In Proverbs 29:18 it is written: "Where there is no vision, the people perish." And we do!

Our being able to hang in there in the difficult times is determined by the nature of our hope. For Christians, it has to do with our holding to the promises of God, a holding that is determined by our confidence in the integrity of God. Here alone our hope rests, as do all of life's possibilities and probabilities. Only in this way can we talk of a hope that does not disappoint us, even if that hope's fulfillment is delayed.

The air terminal was a sea of people, hurrying and pushing. It's always that way. But on this night it was especially so. A snow storm snarled schedules in the air and on the ground. In the midst of the terminal, by herself, there sat a little girl who could not have been more than a first grader in school, six years old, maybe seven. She sat quietly. One might have expected tears, but her big eyes never closed. Wide-eyed she watched. Now and again she smiled. A security guard spoke to her softly, asking if he might be of help. "No," she answered, "I'm waiting for my daddy." She waited for more than an hour. Finally there was a huge smile as she recognized a snow-covered man coming toward her. "See," she said, "I told you he would come." There never had been a doubt. Never did her hope falter. She knew him in whom her hope was fixed. She believed in his love. She believed in his integrity. She knew no storm would keep him from meeting her. And she was not disappointed.

Our "hope that does not disappoint us" must rest always in God's love and his faithfulness.

A Hope Deferred

Keeping that hope focused and vibrant was a great challenge to the first-century Christians. They had expected an early return of the risen and victorious Lord. There was an urgency about their preaching and their missionary work. Christ was coming soon, they believed. By the time Luke set his hand to writing the gospel that carries his name, 40 or perhaps 50 years had passed since the crucifixion. It was the late first century when the evangelist was writing, sometime between 70 and 90 C.E.[2] Many (and supposedly conflicting!) accounts already had been written. There was need to gather information from eyewitnesses and others and to write an accurate account. Luke considered himself to belong to the "third generation" of Christians. Still Christ had not returned. No longer was anyone sure just when that time would come. Some began to doubt that it would come at all.

"A hope deferred makes the heart sick." When the clarity and urgency of the vision becomes dim, so too does the trust, the commitment, the excitement, and the expectation. Moreover, current events of the first century added to the problem of maintaining vision and hope.

The temple had been destroyed in Jerusalem by Titus and the Roman legions in 70 C.E. after a devastating siege and a fierce burning of the city on the day of its fall. It was as Jesus had predicted. Mark records the prediction, and Luke adds some very specific information to Mark's account,

22

suggesting that Luke had information about the actual event which was not available to Mark at his earlier writing date. With the temple's destruction, Jerusalem had become less and less the center of the church, and Christianity was losing its "Palestinian matrix." Even Luke's own text suggests that he was not familiar with the geography of Palestine.

The church was by this time under steady persecution. In 44 C.E. James the son of Zebedee, and probably his brother John, had been executed by Herod Agrippa I. At least a decade before Luke's gospel, Peter had died in that same wave of persecution. As the Roman legions swept down through Palestine to put down the Jewish revolt, Christians were gathered up into the turmoil both politically and emotionally. The Romans often looked upon Christians as a sect of Judaism. Christians could not see the destruction of the temple, synagogues, and other holy places without remorse and wonder. The times were testing the faith of the church. The hope of Christ's return was central.

At least 20 years earlier, Paul had dealt with the deferred hope of Christ's return in the first of his epistles. Concern had been expressed for those who had accepted Christ, lived in the faith and died before Christ's return. How would it be for them? Had they lost their share of the glory of Christ's return? Vision and hope already were crucial matters of questions in 50 or 51 C.E. Carefully, Paul wrote in 1 Thessalonians 4:17b-18, concluding, ". . . and so we shall always be with the Lord. Therefore, comfort one another with these words."

A Parable Of Reassurance

In this context, the early Christians of the late first century found great usefulness in retelling today's parable about the widow and the uncaring judge. The introduction and conclusion as Luke reports them enabled this parable to address the church's need to be steady and steadfast in hope, depending confidently upon the integrity of God.

On the other hand, this parable is not without problems for readers and students in our time. It joins a company of those wherein Jesus holds up questionable models and motivations as apparent examples for the faithful, parables such as the dishonest steward and the friend at midnight (which is a twin to the parable of the widow and the uncaring judge). Curiously, all three appear only in Luke's gospel.

Questions must surely be raised. Why did Luke include parables such as these? Clearly the gospel writers were selective as decades later they sought to reconstruct the stories about Jesus into gospels that would preserve Jesus' life and teachings for future generations.

The problems were obvious. Surely God is not to be compared to the judge who neither feared God nor regarded man. There is nothing here to commend this judge to us as an example of Christian behavior, nor as an example of the ways in which God looks upon, cares for, or responds to the needs and concerns of the faithful.

A similar problem surrounds the widow's prayers. God is not a "slot machine in which one needs only to insert the coin of persistent prayer."[3] to get what is needed. Neither God's will nor his benevolent providential care is bent by the persistence of our prayers. We shall not expect to "wear out" God's endurance and patience by becoming obnoxiously persistent in our prayers. Perhaps the model of persistence is laudable, but not for the reason the parable offers!

Our problems become still greater when we read in Luke 18:1, "He told them a parable to the effect that they ought always to pray and not lose heart." How is the preacher to explain this parable? What do we have to learn here about our heavenly father or about prayer? Why has Luke chosen to include this parable, even following it with another that suggests models of prayer, the parable of two men who went up to the temple to pray?

Joachin Jeremias believes that Jesus' original focus in this parable was not prayer at all, but rather the vindication of the gospel of God's inclusive love,[4] just as the parable of the two

24

men in prayer was addressed to those who "trusted in themselves that they were righteous and despised others." Though the two men pray, neither is to be held up as a model of piety, or even necessarily of prayer. The good news of God's inclusive love is demonstrated by a lesser to greater comparison. If an unrighteous judge who neither fears God nor regards men will finally give justice, how much more generously and speedily will a righteous and loving Father respond?[5]

Such an answer may address with satisfaction the problem of the judge, but it does little to answer with satisfaction the suggestion that persistent prayer will bend God's will to ours, an impression affirmed and strengthened by Luke's introduction to the parable.

Now there comes a new question. Has God's delay in delivering his suffering church been because the faithful have not prayed persistently enough? How shall we read, "Will he delay long over them? I tell you, he will vindicate them speedily." Does this parable explain to the early church why its hope has been deferred?

The Message Of The Parable
In Luke's Day And Ours

Given the turmoil of their day, first-century Christians had nothing other than the Word of God and the promises of the gospel. For them, everything depended upon the integrity of God. Everything! Hope for vindication and salvation were based in God's love, grace and faithfulness. Without these, they had nothing.

There is little wonder that there are repeated calls to faithfulness and sound teaching. The counsel to Timothy is typical (2 Timothy 3:14, 4:2, 3-5):

> As for you, continue in what you have learned and
> have firmly believed . . . Preach the word, be urgent in
> season and out of season, convince, rebuke, and exhort;
> be unfailing in patience and in teaching. For the time is

*coming when people will not endure sound teaching, but
... will accommodate for themselves teachers to suit their
own likings, and will turn away from listening to the truth
and wander into myths. As for you, always be steady,
endure suffering, do the work of the evangelist . . .*

Understanding these things, the introduction and conclusion given in today's parable — the brackets which contain the story — are the keys which unlock the parable's lesson, both then and now. Jeremias appears not to be wholly wrong when he suggests the story is told to vindicate the inclusiveness of the gospel, but this is secondary to the story's fuller intent.

Moreover, to concentrate on the judge's dilly-dallying and to ask, "Is God like this?" is to miss the point of the parable. The parable is about prayer: "They ought always to pray and not lose heart." The parable is about faithfulness: "When the Son of Man comes, will he find faith on earth?" In light of the deferred hope of Christ's early return as Luke wrote his account, the phrase "when the Son of Man comes" carries huge importance.

The central truth here is the faithfulness of God which gives a solid hope to the people of God. There must be no doubt that God will come. The issue is always "When?" and never "If."

Though the parable is not an allegory, the widow becomes pivotal for us. Widows in New Testament times were symbols of all who were reduced to poverty through no fault of their own. Though this widow had a legitimate claim, the judge appears disinterested. Perhaps he was lazy, or perhaps as a village lawyer who was called upon to "sit in judgment" in these things because it was required of him, he wished or expected that she should offer an "honorarium." Everything was against the widow. The judge appears to be on the side of her adversary, and he cares neither about God nor about his neighbors. She has no money to pay legal fees. Her friends appear silent. She has not even a just judge to whom to look. She has no hope whatsoever. Yet, she continues!

There's the key. The widow has no hope. The judge was not one who cared one whit about either God or duty. She had no reasonable expectation that anything good would ever come from her claim. Still, she continued!

In the days of such turmoil, Christians found great assurance in this story. Never would they have thought of the judge as an example of God. They had God's word in his promises. If an uncaring judge can act, how much more should the people of God, filled with hope, expect God to act lovingly and responsibly in their behalf?

Prayer, that gift of conversation with this faithful Father, becomes God's way of including us in his work. Never our way to manipulate God's will, prayer is, our way of discovering God's will. We have no better example than our Lord's Gethsemane prayer. It is such conversations with God that keep our eyes squarely upon him and upon that will wherein our only hope has always rested. Our faithfulness in prayer has virtually everything to do with whether, when the Son of Man returns, he "will find faith on earth."

Persistence is evidence of faith which gives us hope. If the widow, having no legitimate hope whatsoever, could be constant in coming to the uncaring judge, how much more should we be constant in coming to our Father in prayer? Faith, in the first century and in ours, did not and will not succeed without prayer. Without faith, there is no vision. Weariness comes when hope flags. And hope diminishes when faith in God's promises weaken.

A man in his late 20s or early 30s was at a meeting in a congregation in which unrest had prevailed for a long while. "I'm just tired," he mumbled over and over, shaking his head. A saint of many more years watched for a while and then said, "Young man, if you're tired already, you are not going to make it."

That's the question Jesus addresses in this parable and its conclusion. Are we going to make it? Do we pray constantly, keeping our eyes fixed on him whose will is our guide and

27

whose faithfulness is the root of our hope? Do we live in the faith, expecting great things to happen in our lives, in our congregation, and even in our world? It was a Scottish preacher who once observed that to say something is hopeless is to slam the door in God's face!

Again, it's Lucy who has planned a picnic for the next day. She says to Charlie Brown, "I just hope to goodness that it doesn't rain . . ." Walking away, Charlie answers, "Hoping to goodness is not theologically sound."[6] Charlie's right. "Hoping to goodness" is not sound. Fixing our hope upon God is.

When he comes, will he find us faithful?

Amen.

1. Robert L. Short, *The Parables of Peanuts*, (New York, Harper and Row, Publishers, 1968), pp. 265-266.

2. Joseph A. Fitzmyer, S.J., *The Gospel According to Luke I-IX, The Anchor Bible, Vol. 28*, (Garden City, Doubleday and Company, Inc., 1985), p. 55.

3. Eta Linnemann, quoted by Richard Carl Hoefler, *And He Told Them A Story*, (Lima, Ohio, The C.S.S. Publishing Co. Inc., 1979), p. 171.

4. Joachim Jeremias, *The Parables of Jesus*, S. H. Hooke, Translator, (New York, Charles Scribner's Sons, 1956), p. 115.

5. Joachim Jeremias, *op cit.*, pp. 116-117.

6. Robert L. Short, *op. cit.*, p. 273.

A Lesson From Prayers Overheard

We Watched His Eyes!

It was late New Year's Day when the showdown finally came. The number one and two college bowl teams in the nation were set to fight it out in the Fiesta Bowl at Tempe, Arizona, deciding who would lay claim to being the "Beast of the East" and the best in the nation.

Among those who predict such things, there was agreement that the nation's number one team would remain number one that night. Their passing attack had been unstoppable all season long, and it would remain so. A high-scoring game was predicted. Both predictions were wrong.

A defensive struggle prevailed, and the number one team was upset, beaten. Interviews and national news stories alike toyed with the obvious question: "How did you stop their passing attack?" Several strategies had been employed, such as mixing up defensive formations, intimidating receivers by hard tackling, and of special significance, watching the mannerisms of the quarterback. Careful study of earlier films had discovered that he "telegraphed" the direction of a pass. "How did you stop him?" "We watched his eyes!"[1]

These words may hold the key to our discovery of the "central luminous truth"[2] of the parable about two men who went up to the temple to pray, one a Pharisee and the other a tax collector. The key to this parable has to do with the direction of each man's eyes. But more about that in a moment.

On first reading there seems to be no great mystery here. Blinded by our stereotypes, we have long "known" that the Pharisees were insincere and self-centered deceivers of the people who cared more for the praise of their peers than they did for the providence of God. Similarly the publican, honest and forthcoming in his confession, strikes us as a rather decent sort of fellow whose sincerity, in our opinion, outdistances the deceit of his sideways-glancing neighbor in the temple on that day. Moreover, it is something of "our thing" to root for the underdog. Isn't it so!

Because of our stereotypes, the parable fails to challenge us. We find Jesus' conclusion about justification to be reasonable and we consider appropriate his comment about humility. But for Jesus' first hearers the reactions must have been very different. It is important for us to remember that the parable is addressed to critics of the gospel, those who "trusted in themselves that they were righteous and despised others." The "others," such as those to whom Jesus addressed the gospel, were outside of the accepted definitions of righteousness. Already critics of the gospel, and not at all schooled as we are in the Pauline teachings of justification by faith, they must surely have been shocked.

"Scandalous!" "Outrageous!" "Shocking!" "Unheard of!" All of these were the reactions of Jesus' hearers as they wondered at the pattern of his parables. This was not the first such story. There was the parable about the "good Samaritan," too. The victim of thieves had been left along the Jericho Road, robbed, beaten, and half dead. He was befriended and rescued by a Samaritan. By the time the story was finished, good people like the priests and Levites were the "bad guys" and the Samaritan was the "hero."

Now, here he goes again! This time he is picking on the Pharisees, religious laymen who were the "salt of the earth," "pillars of the community," the kind of material from which strong and healthy communities are built. In Jesus' story, the Pharisee becomes the "bad guy," and the publican, the collaborator with Rome, widely recognized as a thief and an extortioner, "goes home justified." Surely Jesus cannot be serious. "What wrongs has the Pharisee done?" "What reparation has the publican offered?" The answer to both of these questions is, "None!" The people must have wondered. So, too, should we.

Who Were The Pharisees?

"Pharisee bashing" is rather commonplace among many Christians, citing those texts wherein there is controversy and confrontation with our Lord. It's easy to take "cheap shots" about their honesty, sincerity, and motivations for their righteousness. "See how proud and self-centered he is?" we ask. But these attitudes cause us to miss entirely the point of our text. The issue here is neither insincerity nor deception. There is no need to assign negative intent to the Pharisee's prayer. Jesus neither claims it nor implies it. Nor should we.

In Exodus 19:6, the people of Israel are called upon to be a nation of priests. Though laymen, the Pharisees took upon themselves this call, assuming the laws of priestly purity. Their vision and intent were honorable. They were the "Hasidim," pious loyalists who "came into their own" during the exile when the Torah and the observance of the law became the heart of Judaism, since they were cut off from the priestly acts of the temple. They provided the backbone for the Maccabean revolt during the inter-testamental period. Some have argued that had there not been the Pharisees, there may not have been a Jewish community into which the Messiah could have been born. They were the leaders of the synagogues in the diaspora, the evangelists and the teachers of their day. Josephus, the first-century Jewish historian, writes that the Pharisees were a body of Jews known for surpassing the others in observance of piety and the exact interpretation of the laws.

Such a man becomes the center of our parable. He is a righteous man in the terms of the practice of the law. If we question his sincerity or his gratitude to God, we miss the impact

31

and the "central luminous truth." What the Pharisee says in his prayer is true. His is a prayer of thanksgiving. Though it is true that it asks nothing, many fine prayers of gratitude would fall under the same scrutiny, and wrongly so. The first-century Talmud records prayers quite similar to this man's prayer. People of the first century would not have found this a flawed prayer, neither self-righteous nor boastful. He thanks God that he is not like others (and he is not!) and that he has been able to go beyond the expectations of the Torah in two gifts, fasting and tithing (and he has!). This man appears to find joy in fulfilling these duties and thanks God that he has been born into a position of life permitting him this great pleasure of praising God.

Jesus challenges none of these things, and in giving us a prayer so near the Talmud's text, we may believe that Jesus has lifted this moment right out of real and everyday life. Though fasting is required only on Yom Kippur, the Day of Atonement, this Pharisee fasts twice weekly. He tithes all that he gets, even those things such as corn, oil and new wine, items for which tithing was not required since the tithe had been paid by the producer of the products. These are all signal acts of self-denial. Moreover, they are acts few Christians, though usually critical of the sincerity of the Pharisees, are faithful enough or motivated enough to understand as the "joys of serving God."

Were it not for Jesus' introduction to our parable and our long-standing stereotypes of the Pharisees, we would see such a man as upstanding and righteous. The point of the parable is not his insincerity. Jesus does not challenge the man's claims. He presents them as facts. And thus he draws the contrast more sharply for us. Because . . .

The Tax Collector And His Prayer

There is no way that the tax collector in this story can be called a righteous man!

Had they been honest (and they were not), the tax collectors would yet have been despised universally among the Jews. They were collaborators with Rome, the occupying power in Palestine. They sold out their own people to a foreign power and became that power's agents for the taxation of their own people.

Poll taxes and per capita taxes were collected by officials of the state. Customs collections were contracted to the highest bidders and were collected for profit by the tax collectors. Consequently, they had to charge a higher rate. Though these tariff rates were most likely set by the state, the system clearly encouraged fraud and excess taxation. The customs agents could not set the rates of the tax, but they could establish the value of thos items being taxed. Graft was rampant. They made their money by oppressing their own people, especially the poor. Tax collectors were not allowed beyond the Court of the Gentiles in the courts of temple. They were political and spiritual lepers.

Though he necessarily "stands far off," we overhear his prayer. His head is bowed and his hands beat upon his breast, clutching at his heart, the seat of one's soul and of its sin. Holding to Psalm 51, he cries the prayer of a helpless and hopeless man: "God, be merciful to me, a sinner!"

This man is telling the truth, too. He is a sinner! And what's more, he makes no offer either of repentance or of reparation. He cannot offer to repent, for he would have no way to earn a living or support his family. Being the highest bidder, he can hardly drop his rates and still make a profit. If he repents, he must also make reparation of the amount wrongly charged, plus a penalty of one-fifth or 20 percent! Unlike Zacchaeus, who in his repentance goes beyond the law ("Half my goods I give to the poor, and if I have defrauded anyone of anything, I restore it fourfold."), this tax collector offers nothing!

Though our hearts would have to be made of stone to be unmoved by this man's helplessness, he can hardly be the "decent sort of misunderstood underdog" we so readily make of him. His honesty is disarming and his plight touching, but he is what he is, and he makes no offer to struggle with change, not even a little bit. Above all, we must not be caught up in our "foggy-headed thinking" that sometimes nods assent when another says, "Well, I know that I am a thief, but at least I'm honest about it." I ask you, what value is there to an honest thief? Is not a thief by definition dishonest, no matter what his protestations may be to the contrary?

Again, our tax collector has offered nothing, neither repentance nor reparation, other than his significant sorrow at what he is and the prayer of a sinner. But compared to the tithing, fasting, and clean living of the Pharisee, it was difficult for those in Jesus' day, and not a few in ours, to believe that such a prayer surpasses the deeds of the Pharisee. And that is the fulcrum of this parable!

Lessons From Prayers Overheard

"Well, what does it mean?" we ask. "Does the prayer of a sorrowful and helpless soul surpass the good works of a righteous man in God's eyes?" Before we answer our own question, a number of lesser but nonetheless useful observations should be made.

1. **Acts in the name of religion are not always redemptive:** The Pharisee was in the right place at the right time, doing the right things, but it was not redemptive for him. Not every activity deemed "for the kingdom" is necessarily so. According to Martin Luther's *95 Theses* and all the work of the Reformation that follows, not every means of raising money is acceptable, even if it is for the church and the "kingdom." Disraeli urged that we cease trying to cover all of our good with the temple roof.[3]

2. **Prayers offered are not always offered to God:** Jesus makes an interesting observation. "The Pharisee stood and prayed thus with himself." While I do not believe or intend to suggest that this is a major point of the parable, it does

touch upon a sensitive nerve for this pastor. More than once I have wondered whether our public prayers are summaries of the morning sermon or lectures to the conscience of the worshiping community rather than intercessions to our Father. William Barclay quotes an account of a Boston newspaper reporting on a local worship event: "It was the most eloquent prayer ever offered to a Boston audience."[4] So, too, I believe more than a few of our prayers might be reported.

3. **Our agendas are not necessarily God's agendas:** As noted, this parable is addressed to the critics of the gospel, the good news Jesus was preaching. But this parable should establish for us that these critics were solidly religious folk in many cases, even though they did not understand. Those who awaited the Messiah and were critical of Jesus had substituted their agendas for God's. They wanted vindication of their calling as a nation and restoration of their dignity as a people among the nations. They awaited a "day of wrath" when the records would be set straight between the just and the unjust. While they awaited a powerful vindication, God sought a merciful reconciliation, the redemption of his people. That was why Jesus kept company with those outside the definitions of the righteous; those who are well need no physician. Thus, the religious, sincere without a doubt, were at cross purposes with the gospel. Just as God loved the hopeless and the helpless, the Pharisees despised them. That's why the parable is told to those who "trusted in themselves that they were righteous and despised others." "I thank you that I am not like other men . . . or even like this tax collector."

Watch Their Eyes!

But our question remains: "Does the prayer of a helpless, hopeless and sorrowful sinner surpass the sincere and righteous deeds of another in the eyes of God?

Our answer is rooted solidly in the Pauline preaching of justification through faith in God through Jesus Christ. It is not that some of us are good and others bad, but rather that all of us, even the Pharisee in all of his good works, fall short of the glory and the call of God. The Pharisee trusted in himself and in his works, and not in the grace of God. Whenever we measure our works by a standard other than God, we fall into the double-sided trap of either unwarranted pride or dishonest humility.

Rather than looking upward to God, the Pharisee looked sideways to the publican; and there is no question about it, the Pharisee looks splendid when compared with a publican! The demon of pride comes racing in and an unwarranted sense of security reigns in regard to our relationship with God.

Not a few of us believe this is the practice that fuels virtually all gossip. Who ever hears "good gossip?" Feeling insecure ourselves, we look to the failure of others to comfort our own sense of spiritual uneasiness and guilt. It's the, "See, everybody's doing it" syndrome.

Watch the eyes when one prays. To whom are we comparing ourselves? Our Pharisee friend had no sense of need when he looked sideways at the publican. He blocked the light of God by his own shadow of self-importance and spiritual success. Measured against a publican, he was a religious giant. Measured by God, the Pharisee was a pygmy!

Which of us can forget the powerful stories of the moments of the sudden encounter with God's power and presence? There's the story of Simon Peter as the catch of fish announces the presence of the Christ: "When Simon Peter saw it, he fell down at Jesus' knees, saying, 'Depart from me, for I am a sinful man, O Lord.' " And there is Isaiah's cry upon seeing the Lord God in the temple: "Woe is me, for I am lost, for I am a man of unclean lips . . . and I have seen the Lord."

Both were giants of the faith. By standing in the light of the eternal and good God, they sound exactly like the publican — "Lord, be merciful to me, a sinner."

It is not, finally, a matter of one of these two men's prayers and lives surpassing the other. Rather, the message is one that Jesus will return to over and again — the mercy of God.

Hundreds of years before Christ the Psalmist understood: "If thou, O Lord, shouldst mark iniquities, Lord who could stand? But there is forgiveness with thee."

Jesus understood, too. And he would tell stories about that mercy and grace, about a loving Father moved by the hopeless publican, so that he would not be helpless. He would tell about the joy of heaven when the lost were found and the outrushing love of a father when a child was seen in the distance, trying to make his way home. He would talk of the mercy of God, and he would show that mercy, touching the diseased and making them clean, touching the broken and making them whole, calling the dead and giving them life, and in the last moment welcoming a dying man into paradise.

The Pharisee's eyes had been on his neighbor and himself, not on God. The publican's eyes had looked into himself and then cried out to God. The truth was that measured against God, neither of them "had a prayer." The point of today's parable is not whether one man's prayer outweighed another's good works sincerely offered. It is not intended as an example of the preferred postures of prayer. Neither is offered by Jesus as a style for sainthood. The story is about the mercy of God and our dependence on his grace.

One of the two knew it, and he went home "justified," having been touched by the love of God. The other man was equally touched and loved by God, but not realizing how much he needed it, he went home with less, knowing virtually nothing of the peace the publican found, and still not understanding that God's love reaches out to all and despises no one.

---

1. Rick Reilly, "Guts, Brains and Glory," *Sports Illustrated,* Vol. 66, No. 2, January 12, 1987. The 1987 Fiesta Bowl game between the University of Miami and The Pennsylvania State University (Penn State). Penn State won the game.

2. Harry F. Baughman, *Preaching from the Propers,* (Philadelphia, Muhlenberg Press, 1949), p. 3. Dr. Baughman quotes the late Professor Raymond T. Stamm in the use of "central luminous truth."

3. Gerald Kennedy, *The Parables: Stories Jesus Told,* (New York, Harper and Brothers, 1960), p. 118

4.. William Barclay, *The Gospel of Luke,* (Philadelphia, Westminster Press, 1956), p. 232.

The Signs Of Salvation

Would that we could know what Zacchaeus was thinking as he ran ahead of the crowd that day in Jericho! What would he have known or believed about the Galilean preacher? What did he think of the crowds that thronged the streets of Jericho, straining to glimpse the teacher as he journeyed toward Jerusalem? Could he have remembered that more than 500 years earlier Isaiah had promised there would be a day like this? Probably not. Zacchaeus had other problems.

To begin with, he was a short man. He had spent much of his life standing on tiptoe looking over the shoulders of others or peering between the people in front of him. Because he was a man of wealth and an official of the town, one might believe that the crowd would have gladly given him a place at the front of the row. But he didn't ask. Had he tried to push to the front, the crowd would more likely have given him serious bruises than a clear line of vision. They hated tax collectors for at least two good reasons: first, tax collectors, usually customs agents who set inflated values and taxed by the fixed rate, were considered dishonest plunderers of their own people; and, second, they were collaborators with the occupying government of Rome, traitors in the minds of the many who longed for Israel's independence and glory.

Zacchaeus was a "chief tax collector" and he had become rich. The crowd would believe, rightly or wrongly, that he had become so at their expense.

It's no wonder Zacchaeus ran ahead of the crowd to a sycamore tree. The tree would give him the height he needed to catch a glimpse of the Galilean, and the protection he needed from a not-so-friendly crowd. With their eyes fixed on the coming procession, they might never look up at all. They might never see him.

After all, trees are great places for hiding, for seeing without being seen. And since we cannot know what it was that drove him to venture into the crowd that day, we do wonder. In the security of his tree, he might even have been a "spectator follower" of the preacher . . . a "treetop saint," if you will.

Now we all know about "treetop saints." We have been there ourselves once or twice, not quite yet ready to say "yes" to the movements and opportunities that were swirling around us. That may be where Zacchaeus was that day — curious but not yet convinced, driven but not yet converted. A few years ago the comedian Flip Wilson was asked about his religious affiliation. "I'm a Jehovah's Bystander," he answered. "They asked me to be a Jehovah's Witness, but I didn't want to get involved."

In the serenity of his tree, Zecchaeus was secure from the unfriendly crowd. They never looked up. He might have been safe from an encounter with the preacher as well. But not on this day. Jesus looked up!

"Zacchaeus!" Jesus called. "Hurry up and come down. I must stay at your house today." Not only had Jesus seen him in the tree, but he had called him by name. He knew his name! When this day had begun, Zacchaeus was up a tree in more ways than one. When it was over, his feet would be solidly on the ground, perhaps for the very first time in his life.

Instantly he was down from his perch. Surely he did not think of it then, but what had begun to unfold for Zacchaeus and the people in Jericho was something the prophet Isaiah had spoken of more than 500 years before. For Zacchaeus, this was the moment of God's fulfilling of a promise.

The spirit of the Lord God is upon me because . . . He has sent me to bring good news to the oppressed, to bind up the broken hearted, to proclaim liberty to the captives, and release the prisoners . . .

I will greatly rejoice in the Lord, my whole being shall exult in my God, for he has clothed me with the garment of salvation, he has covered me with the robe of righteousness. (Isaiah 61:1, 10a).

To Bring Good News To the Oppressed

Suddenly the crowd seemed to be gone. Face to face, just two people mattered. Jesus was looking squarely into the eyes of Zacchaeus. In that moment God had invaded Zacchaeus' life and he would never again be the same. Two things stand out for us here. There is the movement of God and there is a clear new light on the captive and oppressed nature of the life of a man who thought he had everything. Zacchaeus was a wealthy man, but not a rich man, and he was far from free. First, there is Jesus.

Through Jesus, God walked squarely into Zacchaeus' life. We speak so often about our searching for God. The biblical truth is that God comes looking for us. Since the days of Adam and Eve it has always been so. When Moses encountered the burning bush, God became involved personally in effecting the exodus of the Hebrews from the slavery of Egypt. "I have seen the afflictions of my people . . . I have seen their sufferings. I have come down to deliver them out of the hand of the Egyptians." Later, God revealed himself to Moses as "merciful and gracious, slow to anger and abounding in steadfast love for thousands, forgiving iniquity and transgressions and sin."

By the time of the Babylonian deportation and captivity, the exilic prophets Ezekiel and Isaiah were revealing God's active involvement in the salvation of his people:

Behold I, I myself will search for my sheep and will seek them out . . . I will seek the lost and I will bring back the strayed and I will bind up the crippled, and I will strengthen the weak (Ezekiel 34:11, 16).

The lost, the strayed, and the outcast have always been the focus of God's redemptive and reconciling activity. Of all the gospels, Luke brings us this message with intentional clarity. T. W. Manson calls Luke's gospel the "Gospel of the Outcast," and rightly so. God comes looking for us and finds us, even in trees along the streets of Jericho.

Jesus encountered Zacchaeus as he was passing through Jericho on the way to Jerusalem. Luke begins the record of this journey at the 15th chapter, and it concludes with this special encounter. All along the way Jesus was deliberate in his outreach to those the righteous seemed always to have excluded, both then and now.

> Now the tax collectors and sinners were all drawing near to him. And the Pharisees and the scribes murmured saying: "This man receives sinners and eats with them" (Luke 15:1-2).

Jesus answered the charge in the famous trilogy of parables about lost persons and things: the Lost Sheep, the Lost Coin, and the Lost Son. Each concludes with joy in heaven over the repentant sinner. In the course of Jesus' travels, his teaching and preaching speak eloquently of the inclusiveness of God's redemptive work. Parables told along the way include the parables of the Dishonest Steward, the Unjust Judge, the Rich Man and Lazarus, and the Pharisee and the Publican. Each addresses the gospel's outreach to those who would be outcasts. Ten lepers are healed, one a Samaritan. He is the only one returning to give thanks. And now as Jesus passes through Jericho, he calls out to the chief tax collector, Zacchaeus.

It is as if Jesus has taken for himself the prophecy of Isaiah: "The spirit of the Lord is upon me to bring good news to the oppressed . . . and to proclaim liberty to the captives." Christ came to Jericho on that day bringing the good news.

To Proclaim Liberty To The Captives

No one would have called Zacchaeus a "captive"! He was a wealthy man who had risen to the top of his profession in an important city. Jericho commanded the roadways to Jerusalem from the east and the crossings of the Jordan River to the area of Trans Jordan. The importance of the location is attested to by the three sites visible today. There is a modern Jericho, a New Testament Jericho, and the Old Testament site named Tel es-Sultan. The fresh and generous spring known as "Elisha's Spring" is the largest in Palestine. It transforms the area into an oasis in the midst of the parched no man's land of the Judean countryside. Jericho's very name comes from the beauty and bounty of its plants and fruits. Even in ancient times it was known for its rose gardens, dates, balsam groves and tropical fruits.

Zacchaeus had done well for himself in this productive and bustling community of commerce. Josephus, the first-century Jewish historian, calls Jericho "the fattest." Since his "collections" were most likely customs, and the roads for which Jericho served as the "tollhouse" were both strategic and busy, he should have done well . . . even as an honest tax collector, which he may well have been. In his enthusiastic conversion, he says, "If I have defrauded anyone of anything . . ." He does not suggest that he is aware that he has.

He is a wealthy and prominent man. Hardly can one call him a captive. As a chief tax collector and a wealthy man, oppressed seems less appropriate still. Nonetheless, both describe him well.

Prominent and wealthy, he is nonetheless an outcast. As a tax collector he is stereotyped and assumed to be dishonest, whether he is or not. He is captive to the image if not the behavior. Though he is a son of Abraham, he is unable to enter with other Jewish men into the inner courts of the temple for prayer. As a tax collector, a publican, he must stand afar off in the outermost Court of the Gentiles because he is considered a traitor to his country and a plunderer of his own people. To be a tax collector is to be a sinner.

Though Jericho is an important, busy and sizable city, Zacchaeus cannot roam the streets as a free man. It is not so much that he is in fear of bodily harm, but rather that he is shunned by the people. His presence is unwelcome. He is not wanted there. He is alienated from his own people. That may well be why he ran ahead of the crowd and climbed a tree. No one was likely to have cared whether he saw the Galilean preacher or not. That's just it: No one cared at all for Zacchaeus. They abhorred him! They would have taken pleasure in seeing to it that he did not see the Galilean.

No wonder he was so determined to see this preacher. Zacchaeus was not a happy man. Zacchaeus had learned that "however far you go, it is not much use if it is not in the right direction."[1] Wealth means little when one is alone and without self-esteem. It has been wisely said that "we can never attain the self-containedness we so impiously desire. We can live in forgetfulness of him, but not with peace of mind. We can live without his blessing, but not without his judgment."[2] Zacchaeus had alienated himself from God. Just as the tax collector in Jesus' parable, he is trapped by his profession and by his wealth. Even Jesus had said it would be easier for a camel to go through the eye of a needle than it would be for a rich man to enter the kingdom of God.

So here is Zacchaeus . . . up a tree in more ways than one:

> . . . *the rich man who doesn't have a camel's chance of getting into the kingdom of God,*
>
> . . . *the rich man who has everything except public respect, self-esteem, and quiet in his soul,*
>
> . . . *the tax collector whose employers are the very ones who will carry out Jesus' crucifixion . . .*[3]

Jesus calls this man by name. "The Spirit of the Lord is upon me to bring the good news to the oppressed . . . to proclaim liberty to the captives." Zacchaeus! Hurry up and come down. Come out of your hiding. I must stay at your house today."

Clothed Me With Salvation — Set Free

The ancient prophet had said this day would come. Jesus announces it in Zacchaeus' house. "Today salvation has come to this house . . . for the Son of Man came to seek and save the lost." Jesus' announcement is the answer to the grumbling crowd that would wish the gospel to reward the righteous and punish those who are beyond the usual pale of social respectability.

Clearly "salvation" is the goal of God's plan for his Son, Jesus Christ, and this salvation is an important part of the Christ event. Among the synoptic gospels, Luke is the only one to assign to Jesus the title "Savior." Paul writes of awaiting and working out our salvation. For Luke, salvation is something already achieved. "Today salvation has come to this house."

The ancient Hebrew root word most often associated with salvation can be translated "to become spacious, or to enlarge." It is the opposite of being confined, constrained, or oppressed. To "be delivered," therefore, means to enlarge the space in our lives. For Zacchaeus it meant no longer having to hide from God nor fear to walk the streets. Just as alienation creates tensions in relationships and closes doors to people, places and opportunities for us, so salvation enlarges the space of our freedom. It opens all the doors that alienation has closed. Jesus said, "I came that they may have life, and have it abundantly."

Zacchaeus was delivered from his slavery to the "things" he had accumulated. He was free to live creatively, using the things accumulated rather than allowing himself to be used by them. The late Dag Hammerskjold wrote: "You are liberated from things, but you encounter in them an experience which has the purity and clarity of revelation. In the faith which is 'God's marriage to the soul,' everything, therefore, has a meaning. So live, then, that you may use what has been put into your hand . . ."[4]

In a few brief hours, Zacchaeus' life has changed dramatically. He will never be the same man again. Moments ago he was an outcast from God and his own townspeople, running ahead of a crowd that may well have been hostile, climbing a tree to catch a glimpse of a man who might have for him the answers. Salvation had come that day to his house!

Covered With The Robe Of Righteousness
— A Life Changed

Abundantly free, the effect and evidence of salvation is immediate for Zacchaeus. Confronted by Christ, called down from his tree, and with his feet firmly on the ground, Zacchaeus responds with a new excitement and freedom. No longer either oppressed or constrained, even by the law of God, he goes in his new and abundant freedom beyond the mandate of the law:

> *Behold, Lord, the half of my goods I give to the poor; and if I have defrauded anyone of anything, I restore it fourfold.*

The ancient law required a repayment of double the value if the goods were taken in robbery, but only the value of the goods plus a penalty of 20 percent if the confession was voluntary. In either case, Zacchaeus went far beyond the law. In his gifts to the poor, his vision and caring were extended. In the offer of restitution, his sense of justice was affirmed. Clearly, salvation had come to that house that day!

Though Isaiah's reference to the "robe of righteousness" is properly applied to the servant about whom Isaiah speaks, it is correct to say that Zacchaeus, too, was clothed with the robe of righteousness. Always the word has two dimensions: the vindication that comes from God's grace and the quality of life the "redeemed of God" celebrate in their freedom.

Martin Luther writes, "Let everybody regard baptism as the daily garment which he is to wear all the time. Every day he should be found in faith and amid its fruits . . . If we wish to be Christians, we must practice the work that makes us Christians."[5]

Righteousness is the robe God gives, but wearing it is an intentional act of the redeemed. "One's testimony is utterly useless," writes Barclay, "unless it is backed by deeds that guarantee its sincerity. It's not a mere change of words that Jesus demands, but a change of life." Just so, Zacchaeus is determined to bear testimony to his salvation, going far beyond the law.

Solidly On The Ground

Would that we knew what Zacchaeus was thinking — or expecting — as he hurried along ahead of the crowd, climbed a tree and watched for the one about whom he had heard so much. Was he an unhappy man who hoped against all hope that the preacher had an answer for meaning in his life? Was he curious, like so many others? Is it possible that he was a secret follower of the Christ? Had he climbed the tree to avoid the crowds or the Christ? Is it possible that all along he was a "spectator follower" of the preacher . . . a "treetop saint?"

Were that so, he would not have been alone either then or now. There are those who enjoy the security of the perch, either cowering in self-guilt or celebrating the scene and shouting a cheer now and again. But they never march in the parade. They are "treetop" followers . . . "grandstand Christians" who talk a splendid game but always watch from afar. They lift no banners, march in no bands, sing in no choirs, chant no prayers and pledge no gifts, albeit they still enjoy seeing the parade and even fashion themselves to be "soul brothers" to the cause. They enjoy seeing, but not being seen. They gather by the hundreds on most congregations' rolls, and no matter how loudly Christ would seem to call, they are not going to come down from the protection of their trees. They celebrate the scene, but not the sharing.

It was not so with Zacchaeus! Jesus called, and he came down joyfully. Jesus the Master had called him by name. Suddenly his life was changed. Nothing could ever be the same again, not ever again. Life and the goods he had accumulated changed their meanings. "Lord," he said, "half of my possessions I give to the poor, and if I have defrauded anyone of anything, I will restore it fourfold." He was converted in his thinking and enlightened in his understandings so that yesterday's defrauded became today's winners. One converted and newly-enlightened steward of God's blessings can cause a ripple of joy throughout the world. For the first time in a long time, and maybe for the first time ever in his life, Zacchaeus had planted his feet solidly on the ground.

Over and again Christ comes to our hiding places and our living spaces to offer us the same gift of salvation. He calls the "treetop followers," the "grandstand Christians," and the cowering outcasts alike to accept his visit into their places. Life has its ways of driving us all up trees. Christ offers us a way to come down.

Amen.

1. William Barclay, *Testament of Faith*, (London, A. R. Mowbray and Co., Ltd., 1975), p. 4.

2. John Baillie, *Our Knowledge of God*, (New York, Charles Scribner's Sons, 1939), p. 1.

3. Paul J. Achtemeier, *Proclamation 3*, Pentecost 3, Series C, (Philadelphia, Fortress Press, 1986), p. 42.

4. Dag Hammerskjold, *Markings*, Translated from the Swedish by Leif Sjoberg and W. H. Auden, (New York, Alfred A. Knopf, 1988), p. 165.

5. Martin Luther, "The Large Catechism," *The Book of Concord*, Translated and edited by Theodore G. Tappert, (Philadelphia, Fortress Press, 1959), p. 448.

Captive To The Word Of God

The Zealots had made a courageous stand, holding off General Silva and his elite Roman legion for more than a year. Jerusalem had already fallen months ago, and the mesa named Masada, along the west coast of the Dead Sea, was the site of the last pocket of Jewish resistance.

Come morning, that, too, would change. The wooden walls were burning, and within the day's first light the Roman battering ram would begin again and make its final assault upon the weakened walls and gates.

The leader of the 960 men, women and children who held the mesa was Eleazar ben Ya'ir. During the evening he gathered the men of the garrison together, sharing the hopelessness of the morning's coming battle. The defeat was sure, and with it would come the slavery of the strong, the murder of the children and the aged, and the violation of the women. He gave a long and impassioned speech, urging one last act of resistance to enslavement, one last act of freedom: "Let us die before we become slaves under our enemies, and let us go out of the world, together with our children and our wives, in a state of freedom."

With no other apparent avenues of honor, the men of the garrison gathered their families, and by deliberate plan, they gave up their lives by their own hands, an act of freedom done in a determined preference to slavery . . . so great was the Jewish regard for freedom and their hatred of slavery.

When Silva and his men burst through the walls in the morning, they were greeted with the silence of the dead, and the stunning symbol of the love of freedom. Death had been found preferable to slavery.

This story developed in the aftermath of the destruction of the temple in Jerusalem, as Jesus had predicted earlier.

49

The prediction was fulfilled four decades after Jesus' resurrection and ascension.

A Heritage Of Freedom

To be sure, the flame for freedom burned no less brightly in the souls of the Jewish people during Jesus' time. The command of Moses recorded in Leviticus 25:39-42 was taken quite literally: "You shall not make of him a slave: he shall be with you as a hired servant and as a sojourner . . . for they are my servants which I brought out of the bondage of Egypt, they shall not be sold as bondsmen." Josephus writes about the Jews: "They have an inviolable attachment to liberty, and they say that God is to be their only ruler and Lord."

It is no wonder that the Jews who believed in Jesus responded so quickly when he promised to them the truth that "will make you free." "We are descendants of Abraham, and have never been in bondage to anyone. How is it that you say 'You will be made free?' " they demanded!

It was not true, of course! They had twice been "in exiled captivity," held in a foreign land against their will. In their later history, they had been ruled by others more often than not. Their rulers after the exile included the Persians, the Greeks, the Syrians, and at this moment, the Romans. The foremost of all Jewish festivals is Passover. It celebrates the beginning of the exodus from Egypt, God's mighty act of deliverance from the slavery of the pharaohs.

Some of the most beautiful of the writings of Isaiah and the most challenging words of Ezekiel are the prophetic words promising the deliverance of God's remnant from the exile in Babylon.

And now, of course, even as they are speaking, in today's gospel, they are the subjects of Rome. It was that political reality against which the Zealots of Masada would struggle four decades later.

Our first response is to wonder whether Jesus' hearers are not the victims of a sanitized history. Perhaps they chose not to remember.

How is it then, that they can say to Jesus, "We are descendants of Abraham and have never been in bondage to anyone?" Just as history witnesses to the incorrectness of their claim politically, it witnesses, as well, to the truth of their claim spiritually. Through it all, no nation had been able to break their spirit as a people, their faith, their identity, or their traditions. Time after time they managed to survive the pressures of the ancient world that blended and syncretized religions. Through it all they maintained their faith and identity, preserving their uniqueness among their neighbors and their conquerors. The subjects of many, they became the spiritual slaves of no one. They were descendants of Abraham.

The Truth That Frees

The key to today's text is found in the first words of the lesson: "If you continue in my word, you are truly my disciples, and you will know the truth, and the truth will make you free."

This text, or at least a part of it, is one of the most widely-quoted texts of the Bible. It is a particular favorite of democratic societies and goverments wherein it is presumed that the truth can be known and that a people can govern themselves wisely in that truth.

Unfortunately, the full text is seldom quoted. Knowing the truth does not necessarily make us free. The truth may well incarcerate a guilty person. Given our biases and subjective judgments in a complex society, finding and recognizing the truth is not such an easy task, either. Finally, merely knowing the truth does not make us free. Living in the truth we know is what frees us.

This is to say that the opening words of Jesus are pivotal to the truth of the quotation. Note them carefully: "If you

51

continue in my word, you are truly my disciples, and you shall know the truth . . ."

"If you continue in my word" is the condition and, therefore, the text upon which this lesson turns . . . the text which unlocks the meaning of Jesus' conversation with some of the Jews who had believed in him.

It is also important for us to understand the slavery by which Jesus sees the Jews of his generation have been entrapped. What does it mean to be descendants of Abraham? Is it a matter of birthright, a theological pedigree? Do we gain the papers of salvation because we can prove the pure ethnic origin of our birth . . . or even because we revere and hallow the sacred traditions of our people?

Or is a true descendant of Abraham one who shares with Abraham the steady and unshakable faith in God that develops a life of faithfulness, fullness, and a genuine walk in spirit with the "Fathers." All too frequently in the Jews' outstanding history of "survival," they placed their security in the institutions and heritage of Abraham, and not in their love of God and faithfulness to his word and law. As far back as the eighth century B.C.E., the prophets cautioned that God had become weary of the sacred festivals and solemn assemblies. He would refuse to listen to their hymns and their religious music. He demanded justice and righteousness as the heritage of his people, the descendants of Abraham. John the Baptist pulls no punches:

> *You brood of vipers! Who warned you to flee from the wrath to come? Bear fruit that befits repentance, and do not begin to say to yourselves, "We have Abraham as our father:" for I tell you God is able from these stones to raise up children to Abraham. Even now the axe is laid to the root of the trees; every tree therefore that does not bear good fruit is cut down and thrown into the fire (Luke 3:7b-9).*

It is not that we are descendants of Abraham that is the cause of our freedom of spirit, it is — for Jew and Christian alike — that we continue in the Word of God, becoming disciples of him who, whether in the Father or the Son, is the definition of truth . . . and of everything that matters. Jesus' contemporaries were descendants of Abraham, and they had successfully resisted the spiritual slavery of foreign cultures, hostile nations, and human servitude. But they had done so only to be enslaved by their traditions and their heritage, which had finally clouded the importance of God's prophetic word. Correct liturgies and proper parentage became the definitions of their identity. Righteousness and justice, the agendas of God, were displaced.

The Church In The Days Of The Reformation

Let us remind ourselves that those who were Jesus' audience in today's lesson were "Jews who believed in him." This was not a hostile crowd. They were sincere about their faith, even open to new insights and means of spiritual growth. Still, they were slaves to a system that carried God's name and claimed his approval, but was not about his agendas. There's an old saying: "It happens to the best of us." It is well for us to remember this, lest we criticize others without charity and fail to keep vigilance in our own souls. Isn't it so!

Just as the institutions of Judaism of the first century had been caught up into a centuries-old struggle for survival in a world that was secularly and politically hostile, so the Roman Catholic Church had been caught up in issues of spiritual and secular concern. The church was as institutionally defensive and protective of its traditions and authority as were the Sanhedrin and priests of Jesus' day.

While the church held unchallenged control in Europe, the armies of Islam were knocking at the doors of the European states. After the Turks conquered Constantinople in 1453, they marched across Europe, even into the Balkans. The Vatican was called upon to coordinate the effort to defend Christendom and to finance it from a treasury already sorely strained to pay for the building of the Basilica of Saint Peter in Rome.[1]

Pressured by politics, the military threat of the Islamic armies, and an empty treasury, institutional survival and internal discipline were high priorities for the church. When Bishop Albrecht of Mainz petitioned the Vatican for advancement to archbishop, offering a very generous gift to the church in "appreciation," the offer proved to be impossible to refuse. In order to raise the money for the gift, the new archbishop sought a loan and was then allowed to sell indulgences to repay the loan and to assist in the building of Saint Peter's Basilica. Intricate arrangements were made with the Roman Curia, the Fugger Banking House in Augsburg, and the bishop for the payment of the gift and the raising of money to repay bishop Albrecht's loan from the Fuggers. There is reason to believe that these indulgences for the forgiveness of sins were well beyond the church's usual definitions and guidelines.

Dr. Eric Gritsch writes: "The debate over indulgences was not a 'trifling thing.' Rather, it disclosed deeply rooted problems in medieval Christendom, ranging from questions of theological method to authority in the church and the world."[2]

The church had become enslaved to its institutional traditions and its fiscal and political troubles. The Word of God, by which the church was established and for which it was called, was not at that moment the center of the church's concern. There was no readiness to hear a parish priest and university theologian who "spoke out of love and zeal for the truth and the desire to bring it to light."[3]

Continuing in the word of truth was not always the clear priority in the first century. Nor was it so in the 16th century. Even God's faithful can become enslaved by something other than the Word.

Jesus said: "If you continue in my word, you are truly my disciples, and you will know the truth, and the truth will make you free." Luther said at the Diet of Worms: "My conscience is captive to the Word of God." The Word became central in Reformation theology and the theme of its hymns. Today's text was of particular significance, a "reformation text."

Captive To The Word Of God

Continuing in the Word, with our consciences captive to the Word of God, is no small task. Nor is it just the jargon of theologians and preachers. It is the substance of our life in Christ and of our discipleship.

We, too, become slaves of our denominational traditions, our culture, and our local religious patterns. This is so even though we are believers in Jesus Christ, just as those in today's lesson.

The "reformation" must never be allowed to become a 16th-century event. Reformation, the Spirit's work of renewal, is a healthy and needful process of renewal that must be ongoing. Every person in every generation must stand honestly before the biblical evidence, intentionally seeking to "continue in his word," to be captive to the Word of God rather than to denominational traditions, culture, and old local customs.

Our consciences must be captive to the Word of God! Just two years ago, for example, the church council of Saint Luke Evangelical Lutheran Church in Silver Spring, Maryland, determined to participate in an overflow shelter program for the homeless during the coldest months of the year. The congregation would provide for the homeless and street people two meals, showers, laundry, conversation and a warm place to sleep.

Failing to understand the homeless, either the people or the cause, and surely intimidated by a person-to-person, hands-on relationship with those so different, a great uneasiness developed within the congregation. Every possible disaster was imagined, including the fear of the spread of disease. Some members openly spoke of leaving the congregation.

In one such conversation, a member of the council reached for a Bible and softly read to the group the words of Christ:

> *I was hungry and you gave me food, I was thirsty and you gave me drink, I was a stranger and you welcomed me, I was naked and you clothed me . . . Then the*

righteous will answer him, "Lord, when did we see you
. . .?" And the King will answer them, "Truly I say to
you, as you did it to the least of these, my brethren, you
have done it to me (Matthew 25:35-40)."

Slowly the councilman laid the Bible aside. And softly
again, he spoke: "Our consciences are captive to the Word
of God!"

There are many agendas of God in our time. World hunger, peace, ecumenism and the visible and functioning unity
of the church as the Body of Christ in our time surely head
the list. Our family, our friends and our world hunger for the
gifts of grace and reconciliation. Learning and giving the gift
of forgiveness in our congregations and our homes should be
for us a goal and a prayer. Questions concerning racial and
social justice, human sexuality and abortion might appear altogether different if we begin our discussions not from current political or sociological biases and buzz words, but from
the Word of God.

Though many of us have belonged to one or another of
the churches of the Reformation all of our lives, not all of us
have yet learned that we are in daily need of renewal. Though
we love our traditions and the identity we have found there,
it is far more important for us to find our identity in Christ
who is our Lord.

It's no wonder the Reformation churches have placed such
a high priority on the Bible as the sole rule of faith and practice, or why Bible study has been so widely encouraged. We
must daily lay his Word alongside our lives as a measure of
all we have ever thought and a direction toward the things we
do not yet understand.

Jesus said to the Jews who believed in him: "If you continue in my word, you are truly my disciples, and you will know
the truth, and the truth will make you free."

Martin Luther, standing before the Diet of Worms and before Charles V, Emperor of the Holy Roman Empire, said:
"Unless I am convinced by the testimony of the Scriptures

56

or by clear reason . . . I am bound by the Scriptures. My conscience is captive to the Word of God."

What else might it mean to "continue in Christ's Word" and to be his disciple?

> *Lord, keep us steadfast in your Word;*
> *Curb those who by deceit or sword*
> *Would wrest the kingdom from your Son*
> *And bring to naught all he has done.*

> *O Comforter of priceless worth,*
> *Send peace and unity on earth;*
> *Support us in our final strife,*
> *And bring us out of death to life.*[4]

1. Daniel Oliver, *The Trial of Luther,* Translated by Jon Tonkin, (Saint Louis, Concordia Publishing House, 1971), pp. 1-4.

2. Eric W. Gritsch, *Martin — God's Court Jester: Luther in Retrospect,* (Philadelphia, Fortress Press, 1983), p. 19.

3. *Ibid.* Dr. Gritsch gives us here Martin Luther's own definition of his intent.

4. Martin Luther, "Lord, Keep Us Steadfast in Your Word," Stanzas 1 and 3, *The Lutheran Book of Worship*, (Minneapolis, Augsburg Publishing House, 1978), Hymn 230.

The Glorious Company

Harmless fun some call it. Others suggest it is never harmless or funny to joke about evil, even if we know that the witches and gremlins, devils and werewolves who roam our streets are the little children of our neighborhood, and the glaring faces in our windows are no more than hollowed-out pumpkins whose candles will not even last the evening.

While there are some October Scrooges who bemoan the knocks at the door, there are many more who pile up the fruits and candies, turn on the lights and wait by the door for the little ones and their anything-but-frightening, "Trick or Treat!" We chuckle as we listen for the familiar voice from behind the mask, and we drop an apple in the extended bag. Except for a few roaming older teens and perhaps a few soaped windows at their hands, no one worries about the "tricks" that are threatened.

Halloween takes its name from All Hallows Eve, though its origins are pre-Christian and probably go back to the ancient Druids who, with ceremonial fires and legendary visits of ghosts and gremlins, marked the first day of winter on November 1. Others hold that people in the Middle Ages believed that the souls came back and celebrated through the town on the night before the mass for all saints.

No matter. Whatever we think about our Halloween customs in the last decade of this 20th century, there ought to be just a touch of sadness that the day following, a special festival of the church, is all but forgotten in most churches and totally unknown in others.

Martyrs, Prophets And Saints

From the beginning the church has addressed the need to recall with thanksgiving the lives and witnesses of faithful women and men, known and unknown, who have accepted with devotion the call to the gospel of our Lord Jesus Christ, saints all who read the Beatitudes of Christ as a means to bring the kingdom's grace into their world.

The earliest reference to such a day is a feast day for all martyrs of the church, observed in the fourth century by Saint John Chrysostom, Bishop of Constantinople. As a pastor of a congregation in Antioch, prior to becoming the bishop, he delivered a sermon annually on this topic on the first Sunday after Pentecost. By the seventh century such a day was observed as a holy day throughout the Eastern Church, a feast day for all the saints of the church. In 835, Pope Gregory IV established November 1 as the feast day in the Western Church.

After enduring nearly three centuries of periodic persecution until Constantine's Edict of Milan in 313, the church could name a long list of saints and martyrs of the faith, through whom the faithful found inspiration and models for faithfulness, and for whom a continuing hymn of thanksgiving was appropriate.

The ancient *Te Deum Laudamus* hymn, dating from this same period, continues to be a much-loved hymn across the church today. Though doubted by many scholars today, tradition has attributed this hymn to Saints Ambrose and Augustine on the occasion of Augustine's baptism in 387 C.E. In fact, some of the lines appear in a hymn of Cyprian dated in 272 C.E.[1] Either way, the hymn presents us with a solid eschatological view of the church's fellowship and its ongoing hymn of praise:

> *We praise Thee, O God:*
> *We acknowledge Thee to be the Lord.*
> *All the earth doth worship Thee, the Father everlasting.*
> *To Thee all angels cry aloud, the heavens and all the*
> *   powers therein;*
> *To Thee Cherubim and seraphim continally do cry:*
> *"Holy, Holy, Holy, Lord God of Sabaoth;*
> *Heaven and earth are full of your glory."*

The glorious company of the Apostles praise Thee,
The goodly fellowship of the prophets praise Thee,
The noble army of Martyrs praise Thee,
The holy Church throughout all the world doth
    acknowledge Thee:
The Father of an infinite Majesty;
Thine adorable true and only Son;
Also the Holy Ghost, the Comforter.[2]

This fourth-century hymn celebrates the family of Christ to be as wide as the world and as long as eternity! The glorious company, the goodly fellowship, the noble army, and the holy church throughout all the world are gathered into the church's proclamation, its prayers and its song. It is always so, of course. On this day, however, it is especially so! This is the Festival of All Saints, those in heaven and those yet among the living on earth.

The Beatitudes: Guidelines For The Faithful

For centuries the Beatitudes have been associated with this day. They turn the values of this world upside down. The call to live by the standards of the kingdom appeared to provoke attacks upon the just lives of the saints and martyrs of those first three centuries.

Luke, in contrast to similar verses in Matthew's gospel, draws the contrast boldly for us in today's lesson. We have here four beatitudes and four corresponding woes.

Blessed are you poor . . .
    Woe to you that are rich . . .
Blessed are you that hunger now . . .
    Woe to you that are full now . . .
Blessed are you that weep now . . .
    Woe to you that laugh now . . .
Blessed are you when men hate, revile, and cast you out
    Woe to you when all men speak well of you.
                            (Luke 6:20b-26a)

61

Were the faithful of God asked to be no more than the poor, the hungry, the weeping and the victims of prejudice and persecution, that would appear quite enough. Yet, Jesus goes on!

> Love your enemies, do good to those who hate you, bless those who curse you, pray for those who abuse you. To him who strikes you on the cheek, offer the other also; and from him who takes away your cloak, do not withhold your coat as well, . . . and as you wish that men would do to you, do so to them (Luke 6:27-31).

Not only were the people of God to accept poverty, hunger, mourning, alienation and ridicule, but they were to work intentionally to do acts of love and reconciliation for the very ones heaping upon them the injuries and insults! By all standards of our imagination, such an ethic is neither sane nor realistic. Which of us could ever hope to do these things? The answer is clear. It is somewhere between few and none!

But hold on! In those early centuries it happened all the time. It had begun on Good Friday, shortly after noon, "Father, forgive them, for they know not what they do." Shortly thereafter, Stephen, the first martyr after Christ, would raise the same prayer of intercession as he was stoned to death. Virtually all of the apostles would die as martyrs, and Peter, pleading that he was not worthy to die in the same manner as his Lord, was crucified upside down.

From the persecution of Nero onward, Christians would become foils for gladiators, food for lions and even human torches, being burned alive for the amusement of the people. Some emperors were harsher than others, and so the policy of persecution was enforced with more or less enthusiasm. However, persecution swept in waves over the church throughout the first 300 years of its history.

The Beatitudes were their encouragement and their guidelines. Clearly some could accept the challenge better than others. There were enough who did, however, that this widely scattered, regionally divided, theologically diverse, and still emerging group of believers kept the faith within the body and managed in a relatively brief time to convert a whole empire by their faithfulness and courage.

As unreasonable as the Beatitudes sound to us in our day, the early Christians sought to govern their lives by them. Undoubtedly, none accomplished every jot and tittle of the outline. Not all were poor or socially alienated. Some failed the test of courage, surely. Such faith is always a gift of God's grace. We can pray for it always, but we cannot force it from within.

By the time of Constantine, the church had more saints and martyrs than it could name. There was clearly hunger among the grateful and the faithful to have a special festival day of thanksgiving.

Who Follows In Their Train?

Reginald Heber's moving hymn from the early 19th century — a hymn prepared for Saint Stephen's Day — poses the contemporary question, "Who follows in their train?"[3] How do we hear the Beatitudes in our day?

A friend once said, both humorously and honestly, "I am beaten by the Beatitudes. I feel totally overwhelmed." Frankly, I find that a more honest approach to the spirit of these teachings of our Lord than that of hanging them as a piece of framed needlework on the wall, or using a pleasant sentence or two on the front of a greeting card to the bereaved. Nor is this preacher much impressed with those who applaud them but never apply them. They are, finally, hard sayings!

With that in mind, let us make some observations about what they are and are not, developing thereby an appreciation for their use in our time for the building up of the body of Christ, the church, and for finding in them a more abundant life. After all, the best translation for "blessed" is "happy." How can we do all these things and be "happy"?

1. Jesus addressed these blessings, woes and exhortations to the disciples and not to the crowd, as is the case in Matthew's account. The Beatitudes were not initially for everybody. They were intended for the disciples, those who were being set apart to be witnesses of the gospel as apostles. They presuppose the needed grace of God to fulfill their calling.

2. Each of us has different gifts. Not all of us are called to die for the faith, but we are called to live it to the fullest level of trust our gift of faith allows. Faith is finally God's gift to us. We cannot self-generate faith. We should feel no guilt when faith flags. Instead, we should turn to fervent prayer, asking for faith sufficient for the trial.

3. Jesus appears to show little concern about whether the disciples can hear and appropriate this difficult and demanding ethic. Only insofar as they are "in Christ" will they be able to respond affirmatively. God's grace enables us. The point is not that the Christian life is necessarily sad, poor, broken and beaten. The issues are love for the kingdom and trust in the promises.

4. Luke's account, even though the word "now" appears here, should not be interpreted as a "suffer now, celebrate later" theology. While the blessings (happiness!) of heaven await all the faithful through the promises and mercy of God, the issue is one of trust in God which brings peace and purposefulness to the believer. Crusades call upon their pilgrims for huge sacrifices, and yet they are invigorating and even fun. It is always a blessing to stand with someone for something. Let that someone be God and that something be the kingdom! It is written in Psalm 1:

> *Happy are those who do not follow the advice of the wicked,*
> *Or take the path that sinners trod,*
> *Or sit in the seat of the scoffers:*
> *but their delight is in the law of the Lord,*
> *and on His law they meditate day and night.*
> *They are like the trees planted by the streams of water,*
> *which yield their fruit in their season.*
> *And their leaves do not wither.*
> *In all they do, they prosper.*

We Remember With Thanksgiving

It is not a gracious thing the church does on All Saints' Day; it is a necessary thing. It is for us the historic All Saints' and All Souls' Day in one. We give thanks to God on this day for the likes of Stephen, Polycarp, Huss, Luther, Bonhoeffer, Martin Luther King, Jr. and hosts of others, named and unnamed, those canonized in the gratitude of the church and the countless millions who have been faithful over the centuries.

We remember with thanksgiving the parents who brought us to the baptismal fonts and first told us about Jesus. We also remember Sunday church school teachers for the faith they shared by their example as well as their lessons and sometimes even in spite of the lessons.

We give thanks for the witness left with us by the saints, encouraging us onward, proving by their lives that the kingdom can come with power in our lives here and now, and it can change for the better countless thousands.

The martyr first, whose eagle eye
Could pierce beyond the grave,
Who saw his master in the sky
And called on him to save.
Like him with pardon on his tongue
In the midst of mortal pain,
He prayed for those who did the wrong,
Who follows in his train?

A noble army, girls and boys,
With men and women saved,
Around the Savior's throne rejoice,
In robes of light arrayed.
They climbed the steep ascent of Heav'n
Through peril, toil and pain.
O God, to us may grace by given
To follow in their train. [4]

1. Marilyn K. Stulken, *Hymnal Companion to the Lutheran Book of Worship,* (Philadelphia, Fortress Press, 1981), p. 117.

2. E.E. Ryden, *The Story of Christian Hymnody,* (Rock Island, Augustana Book Concern, 1961), p. 32.

3. Reginald Heber, "The Son of God Goes Forth To War," *The Lutheran Book of Worship,* Hymn 183, Stanza 3, (Minneapolis, Augsburg Publishing House, 1978).

4. Reginald Heber, *op. cit.,* Stanzas 2 and 4.

Saints Alive!

This is the day when our vision of the church sweeps the horizons of history and of heaven, all at the same time. We embrace with gratitude uncountable yesterdays. They have been the arenas of faithfulness for God and for his people. In these days God has worked our salvation faithfully and with mercy. In these days generation upon generation of the saints have lived and faithfully served, preserving until our day the saving grace of God's Word and sacraments. At the same time, we see the horizon of heaven, the first light of a new day, the dawn of the fulfillment of God's will in all of creation, a day when all creation joins in the hymn: "Amen! Blessing and glory and wisdom and thanksgiving and honor and power and might be to our God for ever and ever! Amen."

This is the day when we call to mind the size and solidarity of the holy church, a community of God's people extending beyond all the usual boundaries of time and of race, culture, language, nationality, partisan politics, human sexuality and even socioeconomic status. It is a day when we remember the whole company of the saints in heaven and on earth, all of God's people who await the coming of our Lord Jesus Christ and a new heaven and a new earth in which righteousness dwells.

This is the day when the church, with a strong affirmation, lays claim to the living hope we have through the resurrection of our Lord, Jesus Christ. We give thanks for the life and witness of all the faithful departed. We have affirmed it before and we affirm it again in the words of Paul: "If for this life only we have hope in Christ, we are of all men most to be pitied."

This is the day when we reach beyond time as we know it, leaping over the open pits of our own graves and the graves of those we love to a new understanding of Easter's resurrection. All Saints' Day is but a further "commentary on Easter," carrying us beyond the good news of our personal survival to the exciting affirmation of God's ultimate justice, history's righteous fulfillment. Can we believe it? There is better news than resurrection! It tells us to what and for what we shall be raised. We shall be raised in the mercy of God to share in the fulfillment of God's righteousness. There is no lost good after all, and things will finally be set right. This is a day that sets into perspective the words of John:

> *Beloved, we are God's children now; it does not yet appear that we shall be, but we know that when he appears, we shall be like him, for we shall see him as he is (1 John 3:2).*

What We Shall Be

It was Easter morning. The nave of Saint Luke would be filled to overflowing every hour from 8 a.m. until noonday. On the front of the bulletin there was a single brief paragraph, strategically placed:

> *There are just two kinds of people here this morning: Those who believe in the resurrection, and those who wish they could.*

Central in the preaching of the New Testament church is the resurrection of Jesus Christ. The religious leaders found him guilty of blasphemy. They accused him of treason as well. Civil authorities believed it expedient to permit his execution. So, the judgment was rendered on the life and ministry of Jesus, the carpenter from Nazareth. The crowd was of one voice: "Crucify him!" And it was done! "He suffered death and was buried."

On Easter God intervened, overruling the decision of the authorities and the crowds, raising up his Christ. The resurrected Christ deputized his disciples: "You are witnesses of these things." He sent them to preach in his name to all nations, beginning in Jerusalem. All the world would be the new jury and the "witnesses would tell the story over and again." So Peter preaches in the book of the Acts of the Apostles:

> But you denied the Holy and Righteous One, and asked for a murderer to be granted to you and killed the Author of Life, whom God raised from the dead. To this we are witnesses (Acts 3:14-15).

Though we find Jesus' resurrection a comforting assurance that death may have some "survivors" after all, the resurrection affirms much more for us.

1. It affirms God's faithfulness. He does what he promises!
2. It affirms the validity of Jesus' teachings — all of them!
3. It affirms God's victory and power over death.
4. It affirms the destiny of believers.

So affirmed, we are rightly counseled to trust God. The writer of the epistle to the Hebrews 11:1 tells us: "Now faith is the assurance of things hoped for, the conviction of things not seen." Such is our trust of God! Isaiah writes: "Trust in the Lord forever, for the Lord God is an everlasting rock . . . In the path of thy judgments, O Lord, we wait for thee (Isaiah 26:4, 8)."

With the affirmations of Easter we are given new meaning and a new urgency for our lives. We are provided with a sense of direction for the faithful: "For if we have been united with him in a death like his, we shall certainly be united with him in a resurrection like his (Romans 6:17)."

A Prologue To Discipleship

Matthew places the Beatitudes at the very beginning of Jesus' Sermon on the Mount, and this sermon comes very nearly at the beginning of his ministry. In the closing verses of the fifth chapter of the gospel, having finished the calling

69

of his disciples, Jesus begins teaching in the region of the Galilee and in the synagogues of that region. People brought the sick to him for healing, and great crowds were gathering from as far as Jerusalem, the Decapolis, Judea and areas beyond the Jordan.

Seeing the crowds, Jesus gathers the disciples and goes up on a mountain. The opening of his sermon appears to be directed only to the disciples, the "inner circle," those who have left everything to follow Jesus. They are being prepared for their discipleship, and for the ministry they will share with Jesus.

> *Blessed are the poor in spirit,*
> *   for theirs is the Kingdom of Heaven.*
> *Blessed are those who mourn,*
> *   for they shall be comforted.*
> *Blessed are the meek,*
> *   for they shall inherit the earth.*
> *Blessed are those who hunger and thirst for righteousness,*
> *   for they shall be satisfied.*

It must have dawned upon them quickly. No mere collection of sentimental platitudes, these sayings were frontal attacks upon most of our assumptions about how things are in the "real" world. The pattern appears to be humiliation now and glory later. Such a proposal makes no sense whatsoever unless God can be trusted to "deliver" on his promises — "his side of the bargain."

As the ministry of Jesus unfolds, it becomes clear that the Beatitudes reflect the style of Jesus' own life and ministry, and what his disciples will be expected to follow. These words become a prologue to the gospel Jesus will preach, the examples he will set, and the counsel he will give. We recall the question: "Teacher, what good deed must I do to have eternal life?" Jesus said to him: "If you would be perfect, go, sell what you possess and give to the poor, and you will have treasure in heaven; and come, follow me (Matthew 19:16, 21)."

On first reading, poverty of spirit, mourning and humility appear to be spiritual virtues in themselves, but it is not so. Underneath each one of the Beatitudes is the call to live our lives in full trust of God. Spiritual "have nots," who know that they have no righteousness of their own, are those who will hunger and thirst for God's righteousness. Because God can be trusted, they shall be satisfied!

It is only when we have this confidence in the promises of God that we can begin to understand (much less consider following) Jesus' example and his mandate. The Beatitudes must be studied in the context of a community of trust, of vision and of hope. Neither platitudes nor political platforms, but they are serious expectations of those who live confidently in the light of Christ, and of his resurrection.

To be disciples of our Christ, we must pray for that solid trust that gladly accepts whatever condition in which we find ourselves as places in which God can and does act. In such matters, our faith in our Father's plans for the future does much to inform and enable the faithfulness of a given moment.

The Work Of Faith

From the first four of Jesus' "Beatitudes," it appears that the followers of Jesus are more nearly "victims" than "disciples." They are the spiritual "have nots" who must trust and depend wholly upon God and his promises. However, Jesus has in mind for us something more than our passively staying out of trouble . . . trusting God, being deeply sorry for the suffering of the world, practicing self-control, and longing for perfect righteousness. The works of faith are not passive. They are active and outreaching.

Now the disciples, solidly established in faith and with a firm hold on God's promises, are free to live in love, being of a single mind (pure heart), showing mercy, and actively doing the hard work of peacemaking, even accepting persecution with purpose and with rejoicing.

Being of a single mind about the things of the kingdom, the disciples are called to be merciful, just as they have received and experienced God's mercy. More than a gracious attitude of good will, "being merciful" includes having empathy for another's suffering and participating with another in setting things aright. It is an act of healing.

So, too, is peacemaking. Making peace involves proclamation, diplomacy, self-control, a willingness to forgive and to promote the work of forgiveness among others. Again, the issue is an active participation with God in healing.

For the Hebrews, "peace" is more than the absence of conflict. *Shalom,* the greeting readily shared in the Middle East today, bids the prayer of "peace." This single-word blessing is always more than a prayer that another be spared from evil and hurtful things. It prays as well that he may be blessed by the presence of all good things. It is sometimes translated: "May all things be for you as God wills."

Jesus' Beatitudes appear to "flow" into the work of peacemaking. Those who do works of mercy and charity, all the while mourning the suffering of the world's brokenness and hungering for righteousness, are by their nature makers of peace. In Saint Augustine's *Summa Theologica* he has written:

> *Peace is the work of justice indirectly, insofar as justice removes the obstacles to peace; but it is the work of charity (love) directly, since charity, according to its very notion, causes peace.*[1]

Confident in God's promises and with a clear hold upon what is promised to come, Christ's disciples endure persecution, slander, and alienation for the sake of the kingdom. Though one is a victim of such activities, a disciple accepts this suffering as an opportunity for the proclamation of the gospel. Saint Paul has written:

> *We are treated as impostors, and yet are true; as unknown, and yet well known; as dying, and behold we*

live; as punished, yet not killed; as sorrowful, and yet always rejoicing; as poor, yet making many rich; as having nothing, and yet possessing everything (2 Corinthians 6:8b-10).

The Charter Of The Kingdom

It should now be clear that the Beatitudes are more than platitudes or impossible rules for another age. In these words the New Testament church recognized the pattern of Christ's own life and pattern of the life that is to be lived in the light of the resurrection and the power of the Spirit. They are not "guidelines" for the kingdom that is coming; they are the "charter" of the kingdom of God that is already here. Insofar as the saints of God commend themselves to our world, these patterns are the evidence of the kingdom's presence and its power.

It's no wonder, then, that the church from the early centuries — as far back as Saint John Chrysostom and his preaching days in Antioch — has set aside at least one day each year to remember with thanksgiving the departed saints who now rest.

At the same time the church lifted these prayers and hymns of thanksgiving, she called to remembrance the lives and examples of the saints for the education, edification and encouragement of the living. Having managed, to a greater or lesser degree, to be faithful to Christ's example, and to his charter for life in the kingdom, these "saints" were an inspiration to all the living. This "remembering" is at once an act of gratitude and of edification. This the church ought to do. And it does!

Saints Alive!

But hold on just a minute. Not all of the saints are dead. Though the original festivals called to mind the martyrs, the known and the unknown, the unnamed and never canonized, there are others to be remembered this day, too. According to the New Testament, the title of "saint" is not reserved solely for the perfect.

Saints are not alone the martyrs, the dead, and the "canonized." The New Testament calls all baptized Christians "saints." It is not a matter of spiritual and moral victories, but a gift of the grace of God that works in Baptism. Though sinners, we have been redeemed and made holy by the grace of God.

The "saints" include the extraordinary and the ordinary, the common as well as the uncommon and the unnamed cloud of witnesses about which the writer of Hebrews speaks (Hebrews 12:1). Moreover, it includes the living as well as the dead. One need not die to be a "saint."

The challenge of life in the kingdom, vividly drawn for us in the Beatitudes, is not solely a definition of the life yet to come, the property of the "saints triumphant," a "code" for the life to come. The Beatitudes are the charter of the kingdom today, here and how.

Living with God's gifts of grace as the birthright of our baptism, we are called, just as the classic saints of old, to struggle with our bewildering time and its confusing issues. The kingdom of God is at hand, and our Lord explained the responsibilities of our citizenship.

A Final Word For The Living Saints

It is not, after all, a matter of earning our salvation, nor of believing that only superhuman piety can prevail. In our baptism, we have God's promise. He has given us his word. We need only cling to it. But then, that's just how Jesus began the Beatitudes in the first place.

O the bliss of the man who has realized his own utter helplessness, and who has put his whole trust in God . . .[2]

This is a day of thanksgiving for all the saints . . . and especially for those who now rest from their labors. The prayer of the church is said again: "May the souls of the faithful departed, through the mercy of God, rest in peace."

We remember them with thanksgiving.

But finally, today's good news, as it is every day, is God! God's grace makes this day one of hope and not of superstition, of joy and not of mourning, of vision and not of dreaming, of truth and not of resignation — a celebration of life that sets aside the dirge of death.

Today is the day we sweep the horizons of history and of heaven, all at the same time. All that happens this day is caught up in this one fact: God remembers. He remembers us and he remembers his promises.

> *He recalls his promises and leads his people forth in joy*
> *with shouts of thanksgiving. Alleluia. Alleluia.*[3]

Blessed are those who trust wholly in God, for theirs is the kingdom of heaven. Indeed so!

1. Myron R. Chartier, "Peacekeepers or Peace Makers," *The Clergy Journal,* Vol. 61, No. 7, May/June 1985, (Austin, Church Management, Inc., 1985), p. 16.

2. William Barclay, *The Gospel of Matthew,* Vol. 1, (Philadelphia, The Westminster Press, 1958), p. 87. This is Barclay's paraphrase of the opening of the first Beatitude.

3. "Thank the Lord," *The Lutheran Book of Worship,* (Philadelphia, Augsburg/Fortress, 1978), p. 115.

Our Living Hope

Not every question requires an answer. Sometimes the hope is that there will be no answer. Questioning can be "posturing," that is, taking a position rather than soliciting information. By the questions raised, information is given as well as asked. Often playing to the audience of listeners or bystanders, questions are intended to manipulate others while vindicating the posture of the speaker. One needs only to listen to a congressional hearing or a political debate to watch masters of an art most of us practice. Isn't it so!

Watching a televised presidential news conference recently, one could not be sure whether the President of the United States was answering reporters' questions or dodging interrogatory missiles. Not at a loss for words, the president did a creditable job of bobbing, weaving, dancing and counter jabbing.

Like a skilled prizefighter, dancing and bobbing, Jesus has been ducking hostile questions, weaving through discussions, and jabbing back with knockout punches throughout this 20th chapter of Luke's gospel. Three times thus far in this chapter, hostile questions have been raised, sometimes as open challenges and sometimes with feigned sincerity. Each time Jesus has turned these combative questions to his advantage.

A Procession Of Opposition

First come the chief priests, the scribes and the elders. This is no mere visit of the temple guard; Jesus is confronted by the highest temple authorities as he teaches. The scribes and elders were members of the Sanhedrin of Jerusalem. Every

Jewish community had its "Council of Elders" which interpreted the law and measured out punishment appropriate to the offenses of the law. But the Sanhedrin of Jerusalem was the "Supreme Court" of all first-century Jewry. The scribes were "a class of professional exponents and teachers of the law." During the exile when the people were cut off from the temple and its worship, the scribes came into their own. They, too, were members of the Sanhedrin. Jesus' challenge by the Sanhedrin is Luke's last recorded occasion of Jesus' teaching in the temple.

Together the chief priests, scribes and elders were the official "guardians of orthodoxy." Their questions of Jesus were obvious and direct. They asked, "Tell us by what authority you do these things, or who is it that gave you the authority?" Before they asked, they knew the answer to both questions or they supposed that they did. Together, they represented the highest religious authority in Jerusalem and in all first-century Jewry. They knew they had not granted him the authority to teach. They were not expecting an answer. They were posturing themselves for the censoring of his activity.

It would appear at first that they had succeeded. Surely Jesus would be defensive, for the official authority to teach was theirs alone to give or to withhold.

Quickly Jesus answers with his own question: "Was the baptism of John from heaven or from men?" He did nothing other than apply their question to John's teaching. If they said it was from heaven, he would then ask why they did not believe and follow John. If they answered that it was from men, then the people might well riot. They could only answer, "We do not know." Quickly Jesus countered: "Neither will I tell you by what authority I do these things."

Jesus follows this encounter with the Parable of the Wicked Tenants, a parable the scribes and chief priests understood clearly. They were angered and would have arrested him. But again they feared the reaction of the people.

Then came a new strategy. Spies were sent, posing as interested followers and sympathizers to the gospel. Again the question was for the purpose of posturing, not for gathering information. They asked, "Is it lawful for us to give tribute to Caesar or not?" Again Jesus dodges their attack. "Show me a coin. Whose image is on it?" "Caesar's," they answer. "Then render to Caesar the things that are Caesar's, and to God the things that are God's." In spite of themselves, they were impressed!

Always the issue was entrapment. Had he said that taxes ought not to be paid, he could be reported to the Roman authorities as a teacher of rebellion. If he suggested accommodation with Rome, he would lose many who longed for the vindication and restoration of Israel's hope and prestige. They raised the questions, but Jesus refused to let their assumptions define the issues.

Resurrection — Absurdity Or Reality?

Now come the Sadducees! They were the party of the high priests and were, themselves, from the priestly and aristocratic families. Josephus reports that they have the confidence of the well-to-do only, and no following among the people. Their teaching has reached but few people, yet these are men of highest esteem.

Representing the high priests, the Sadducees were "ultra-orthodox." They accepted the first five books — the books of Moses — as the only authoritative Scriptures. These books, known as the Pentateuch, had been directed toward a nation of shepherds and nomads. People in Jesus' day lived in an increasingly urbanized Israel. Updating Jewish teaching and piety was primarily the work of the Pharisees. Their different views of Scripture, which books were included and their interpretation, brought great differences between the Pharisees and the Sadducees. One of these differences was the doctrine of the resurrection, one that began growing in popularity during the inter-testamental period and was held by many in Jesus' day, including the Pharisees. About the Sadducee's belief, Josephus writes: "As for the persistence of the soul, penalties in death's abode, and rewards, they do away with them . . . the souls perish along with the bodies."

Now, for a fourth time in this chapter, Jesus is faced with a question. A favorite topic of the Sadducees, their hypothetical story about the eschatological implications of a doctrine of resurrection — given Moses' instruction about Levirate marriage — appears to have no rational answers. For example consider the question: "At the resurrection, whose wife will she be?" For the seven [brothers] had her as wife." They rejected the doctrine because it is nowhere supported in the Pentateuch as they read it. Debating from its implications instead of its merits, they sought to reduce the hope of the resurrection to an absurdity. As the Pharisees had been unable to answer convincingly in the past, they were certain Jesus would have no answer either.

Resurrection — A Living Hope
From A God Of The Living

They were wrong again — twice wrong!

Contrary to what most believe, good answers do not begin at the conclusion of a sound debate. Good answers and accurate truths become possible at the very beginning of the debate, at the moment when the definitions and assumptions are established.

The answer to the hypothetical question of the Sadducees was not to be found in a more cunning conclusion. It was to be found in a careful examination of the assumptions upon which the story was built. In these, the Sadducees assumed too much and too little.

They Assumed Too Much

They assumed too much when they assumed that "resurrection" was a belief in "immortality." That is to say that life has no ending. It goes on forever! "To believe in resurrection is not to say we are immortal." To teach a doctrine of "resurrection" affirms that we are mortal, the price of sin is death. We shall all die.

The Sadducees assumed otherwise. The problem with their argument was not in its conclusion, but rather in its beginning! They assumed that "resurrection" meant life would continue unchanged — as it always had — forever. "On the other side," or "in the new age," we would simply pick up where we had left off in our relationships, responsibilities, and all such. Two things must be observed:

1. Resurrection means that we are "raised again" from the dead. Death is real, not imagined. If we were still living, we would not expect to be "raised."

2. While the Bible is replete in assurances that relationships continue to be functional and faithful in our loving and caring, it is a different body and a different life, as the resurrection narratives clearly suggest and Paul describes.

Our human mortality makes marriage an "order of God's creation" tending to the necessity for the production of the family and of human life. But it is an order of this creation and not of the next. Since there is no more death, there is no needed arrangement for our human sexuality to preserve the race, to express intimacy, or to create new life. Much we do not know about the "new age," much we do know. It will be a time marked with all the blessings and joys of being together in the presence of our Lord. It will be entirely different from what we now know. It will not be a continuation of "business as usual."

Simply put, the question is not Plato's question: "If a man died, is he still alive?" The question is Job's question: "If a man die, shall he rise again?" The answer is Jesus' answer: "The path of glory leads from the grave."

And They Assumed Too Little

The Sadducees assumed far too little about the power, the grace, and the faithfulness of God.

In reply, Jesus refers neither to his coming ordeal and resurrection, nor to the miracles performed that dealt with the issues of life and death. Instead, he carries the Sadducees back into the heart of their treasured Pentateuch, to Exodus 3 and the story of Moses and the burning bush. Here, God is referred to as the God of Abraham, of Isaac, and of Jacob. He is not the God of the dead, but of the living. Further, Jesus draws upon the ancient Jewish theological conviction that the dead are separated from God, which is what makes death so terrifying. At the time of Exodus 3, the patriarchs were long ago dead. But for God to remain their God, they must be living, or at least they are going to be living again.

Setting aside the exegetical technique of a first-century rabbi, Jesus now moves beyond the point of the Sadducees' misunderstanding of the Scriptures to note that they have misunderstood and underestimated the power of God. "All live to God." The power that allows God to create life in the first place gives him the power to raise it up. "All live to him" is to say that no one, living or dead, is beyond the power of God. Paul writes forthrightly in Romans 8:38-39: "For I am sure that neither death, nor life, nor angels, nor principalities, nor things present, nor things to come . . . will be able to separate us from the love of God in Christ Jesus our Lord."

Truth begins in any good debate not with the cunningness of the conclusions, but in the care with which the assumptions and definitions are drawn at the beginning. The Sadducees assumed too much and too little. Though their logic was unassailable, their conclusion was absurd. The absurdity rested not in the doctrine of the resurrection, but in the careless assumptions with which they had begun their consideration. Though logically sound, given their assumptions, they, nevertheless, missed the point entirely.

They assumed far too little about God. They believed that all God was able to do was what they had observed him doing in the past. This attitude is not without merit when we hold so strongly to a doctrine of God's self-revelation, but it becomes almost demonic when it denies God's creativity and his longing for our redemption.

Teacher, You Have Spoken Well

Incredible, isn't it? The chief priests, scribes, elders and Sadducees have on four occasions sought to prove the Christ an imposter, a false teacher of the Jews. They have challenged his authority to teach, and sought to entrap him in treason either to the Jewish hope or to the Roman occupation. They have presented him with an old argument about resurrection that had confounded the scribes and Pharisees for centuries. Those who sought to "catch him" find themselves marveling at his answers. They had intended to "prove" some things about Jesus. They had not expected to learn anything by their carefully crafted questions. Finally, some of the scribes, the "professional lawyers," exclaim: "Teacher, you have spoken well." We agree!

There is but one point yet to be made, and it is this. While the Sadducees made two crucial mistakes because they understood neither the Scriptures nor God, it is important for us to understand that the entire lesson is about God, his power and our faith in his promises.

1. **Eternal Life Flows From God Alone** — There is no encouragement here for a doctrine of human immortality. Death is real for us, biblically and existentially. There is no eternal life without God. There is no eternal hope in the Scriptures except that which flows from the love, power and faithfulness of God. If we are to live eternally, then it is God who must raise us. The dead are dead. They cannot pull themselves up. Only God!

2. **What We Believe About God is Crucial** — We cannot ever begin a discussion of eternal life based upon its logic or its "proofs." Such a discussion always begins with God and our trust of his word. There is no question that the God of creation, who created us in the first place, can raise us up if he wants to. The hope of resurrection is always rooted in our trust of God.

3. Since **"Nothing Can Separate Us** . . . from the love of God," there is no one, living or dead, beyond the reach

of his power to redeem and raise up. There is no grave out of God's reach. In just the same fashion, there is no living person — no matter what that person's alienation or sin may be — who is beyond the reach of God's power to redeem. And that's the best news yet. "He is not the God of the dead, but of the living; for all live to him."

Paul, writing to the Christians at Thessalonica in the first century, provides for this good news a fitting benediction:

> *Now may our Lord Jesus Christ himself, and God our Father, who loved us and gave us eternal comfort and good hope through grace, comfort your hearts and establish them in every good work and deed (2 Thessalonians 2:13—3:5).*

A Plan For Difficult Times

Appropriately Impressed!

They were impressed! Mark's gospel quotes the comment Jesus overhead in the opening of today's lesson: "Look Teacher, what large stones and what large buildings!" The contemporary Roman/Jewish historian Josephus writes that the temple "appeared from a distance like a snow-clad mountain, for all that was not overlaid with gold was of purest white."[1] This temple built by Herod was as massive and awesome up close as it was at a distance.

Though called the Second Temple to this day, it was more honestly the third temple to be built upon this site. Solomon had built the first, constructing a flat platform, encompassing with retaining walls the outcropping of rock that had been Arunah's threshing floor, the location Solomon's father, David, had purchased as the site of the temple. Solomon's temple had stood for 370 years when it was first looted. A decade later, in 586 B.C.E., it was sacked and burned by the Babylonians.

After the exile the temple was rebuilt under the order and patronage of Cyrus, the king of Persia. More modest than the temple of Solomon, the temple was completed under Zerubbabel in 516 B.C.E.

Herod the Great, the paranoid king of the Christmas birth narratives, rebuilt the temple of Zerubbabel. Despite his well-documented crimes and excesses, he was, nonetheless, a master builder whose skills cannot be denied. He determined that Jerusalem would be the most imposing of all of his work, and to win the loyalty and support of his Jewish subjects, he would rebuild the temple as the grandest of all of Jerusalem's buildings.

Building upon and extending beyond the foundations of Solomon and Zerubbabel, he nearly doubled the area of the temple mount, enclosing within the retaining walls an area of 35 acres! While it had taken Solomon's architects and artisans seven years and five months to complete the first temple, Herod's first stage of construction required a decade. The temple itself was begun in 20 B.C.E. and dedicated in 10 B.C.E. But according to Josephus, Herod's 18,000 workmen continued work until 63 C.E.

To enlarge the temple mount to enclose 35 acres, strong retaining walls had to be extended down into the Tyropoeon Valley to the west and down Ophel hill to the south. Ashlars, huge building blocks, were quarried, cut, faced and fitted without cement. All are proportionally large, but the largest measures 46 feet long by 10 feet high and 10 feet deep. Weighing 415 tons, it makes the stones of the Egyptian Pyramids — a mere 15 tons — to be as pebbles![2]

"Noble stones" indeed! This was Herod's *magnum opus*. The Talmud says: "Whoever has not seen Jerusalem in its splendor has never seen a beautiful city."[3] Pliny the Elder, a Roman scholar, writes of Jerusalem as "by far the most renowned city of the Orient and not of Judea only."[4] Josephus writes that the temple is "more worthy of description than any other under the sun."[5] Remarking about the height of the pinnacle of the temple (the southeast corner), he notes that anyone looking down to the Kidron Valley 100 yards below would become dizzy.[6]

Little wonder that Jesus overheard them speaking of the temple, how it was adorned with noble stones and offerings. And it is little wonder that many listened in stunned disbelief when he said on another occasion that he would destroy it and rebuild it again in three days. As Jesus lived, it had already been under construction for 46 years and that construction would continue three decades after Jesus' death!

On this day, however, there is no talk of rebuilding. There's just the terrifying prophecy: "As for these things you see, the days will come when there shall not be left here one stone upon another that will not be thrown down (Luke 21:6)." That day would come just four decades later in 70 C.E. Those who read Luke's gospel knew the details of that day first hand. You see, Luke was writing on the other side of the temple's destruction.

When The Day Came

Sabbath by Sabbath and holy day by holy day, it was the custom of a priest to climb, with shofar in hand, to the top of the southwest corner of the temple mount at the beginning and at the end of the day, announcing both the day and its hour. The sound of this ram's horn could be heard throughout Jerusalem.

But on August 28 in the year 70 C.E., there was another sound. It was the sound of fire. The flames could be seen from Mount Zion (the upper city) as they climbed the pinnacle. Tradition says that this is the very same day that the Babylonians had put the torch to Solomon's temple in 586 B.C.E.

For nearly a month the people of the upper city held out against the siege and the power of Rome. But on September 20 the Romans overran the city, slaughtering the inhabitants and putting the entire city to the torch. Recent archaeological finds in the upper city confirm Josephus' account; in moot silence they give evidence of the fire, the haste and the carnage.

Forty years later, it had happened as Jesus had said. The 40-foot colonnades that surrounded the temple mount, the temple itself, and Herod's huge portico were all gone, pushed down and pulled over, rolling into the Tyropoeon Valley to the west and the Kidron Valley to the east, significantly lifting the levels of both valleys. For the most part, the stones remain to this day right where the Romans left them. Along the Western Wall, often called the Wailing Wall, there remain 25 courses of Herodian ashlars, 14 of which are visible and above ground. In Jesus' time, all were visible. The pinnacle of the temple overlooking the Kidron Valley stands at 141 feet, about half of its original height.

With the exception of these retaining walls, there was not one stone left upon another that was not thrown down. It was just as Jesus had said. The late first-century readers of Luke's gospel knew that it was so! Jesus' prediction had been incredible to the first hearers. When the day came, it was even more so.

When The Stars Begin To Fall

The prophet Malachi said, "Behold, the day comes, burning like an oven (Malachi 4:1)." It would be a day when God's judgment would burst upon the world, consuming the wicked and giving blessing and vindication to the righteous. But when the day came, it seemed that the wicked prevailed. Chaos reigned in communities and in religious life. It was as if the whole world was coming apart and the hope of the righteous dissolving. The old spiritual hymn suggests the disintegration of all of creation: "My Lord, what a mornin', when the stars begin to fall!"

The relentless and methodical manner in which the Romans destroyed the temple, leaving not one stone upon another, was the same manner in which Titus and his legions swept through all of Palestine. Though there were hundreds of first-century and earlier synagogues all through the land, modern archaeological search has not yet discovered a single example of a mid-first-century synagogue other than the one at Masada and another at Herodian, both personal fortresses built by Herod (and both thought to be restored in the late first and early second century).

Christians could take no glee in the devastation. They had been hounded by persecution from the beginning, first by the Jews and then by the Romans. This political and spiritual "ambush" deepened the suffering for Christians who understood themselves in the fullest sense to be Messianic Jews.

All that Jesus had said was as Luke's readers found themselves living it: "They will lay their hands on you and persecute you, delivering you up to the synagogues and prisons, and you will be brought before kings and governors for my sake. . . . You will be delivered up even by parents and brothers and kinsmen and friends, and some of you they will put to death; you will be hated by all for my name's sake (Luke 21:12, 16-17)."

Just as the temple had been the center of gravity for Hebrew identity, worship and hope, holding the "world of the faithful" in a reasonable orbit, now its tumbling stones had become the symbol of the disintegration of the Hebrew heritage on the one hand and the Messianic hope on the other. It was a terrifying time for Christian and Jew alike and may well explain why the Jews saw in Christians a threat and not a fulfillment. Worse still, there was no evidence that the righteous would prevail in either tradition.

The Call To Witness

Jesus' words brought great encouragement to the early Christians. Decades before it happened, Jesus had predicted it. This was no surprise in the timeline of salvation. This was no sudden reversal in the balance of power between God and Christ on the one hand and "the rulers of this present darkness . . . the spiritual hosts of wickedness in the heavenly places, as Paul would name them, on the other (Ephesians 6:12)."

The faithful are not without weapons. Standing with the whole armor of God, we have in our hands the sword of the Spirit, which is the Word of God. Jesus says it like this:

> *This will be a time for you to bear testimony. Settle it therefore in your minds, not to meditate before hand how to answer; for I will give you a mouth and wisdom, which none of your adversaries will be able to withstand or contradict (Luke 21:12-15).*

The enemy can be defeated. God's promises will prevail. These are the times that the faithful are called to stand tall.

"These are the times," as Thomas Paine is often quoted, "that try men's souls." These are the times when the most powerful preaching is done. In the courage of a Stephen, the conversion of a Saul begins. These are the times when Luthers stand before hostile diets having nothing in their hands but the Word. These are the times when Bonhoeffers stand before Gestapo interrogators and compromise nothing.

Not A Hair On Your Head Shall Perish!

Virtually everything Jesus has said has been fulfilled except, perhaps, this one! History is filled with martyrs of the faith, Stephen was the first. The last are yet unnumbered and unnamed. Isn't it so!

But here again, the issue is the promise of God and the destination of the faithful. We are strangers and pilgrims on this earth. By baptism we have been made heirs of the kingdom and members of the commonwealth of heaven. We wait for a new heaven and a new earth in which righteousness dwells. We shall not perish. To perish is to disappear, to cease to be. God has promised otherwise — from the cross: "Today you will be with me in Paradise (Luke 23:43)."

An English officer and a fellow prisoner wrote these words about the last hours of Dietrich Bonhoeffer:

> On Sunday, April 8, 1945, Pastor Bonhoeffer conducted a little service of worship . . . He had hardly ended his last prayer when the door opened and two civilians entered. They said, "Prisoner Bonhoeffer, come with us." That had only one meaning for all prisoners — the gallows. We said goodbye to him. He took me aside: "This is the end, but for me it is the beginning of life." The next day he was hanged at Flossenburg.[7]

But What Does It All Mean

Without a doubt, this is a challenging and yet difficult text for us. We can understand it in its historical context, but what does it all mean for us? We are not likely to stand before diets, be tied to stakes, or to look into the noose of a gallows. And how do we understand the prediction of international wars, earthquakes, famines and the fireworks of the cosmos?

This is a style of writing popular among the Hebrews from the days of the exile and into the first century. There was the belief that the world of this "age" was evil and unredeemable. As the next "age" of righteousness breaks in with God's intervention, the powers of evil will rage until they are finally defeated and the righteous of God are vindicated. There were, of course, many variations on the basic theme. This "apocalyptic" style sought to bring eternal realities into earthly images that could be comprehended in this eschatological drama of the "last things." While prophetic in tone, it was written to encourage the faithful in its day. In the case of today's gospel, virtually all Jesus had predicted has already been fulfilled. Yet, its value then and now is significant because:

1. It believed firmly in God's power and intent to defeat the forces of evil. Folks in our generation have little sense of direction or of destiny. If salvation is believed at all, it is considered "universal."

2. Apocalyptic writings looked seriously upon the powers of evil, seeing a fearful and significant cosmic struggle. The ancient baptismal question is basic: "Do you renounce all the forces of evil, the devil and all of his empty promises?"[8] We are called upon every day to decide, and we need to deal seriously with the "forces of evil."

3. Apocalyptic literature called upon its readers to decide, to stand firm and to join the battle for justice and righteousness. Precisely put, "Whose side are you on?"

All of which is the point to Jesus' answer to the very natural questions of his disciples: "How?" "When?" and "What will be the warning signs?"

Make no mistake, persecution is a fearful thing, be it political or spiritual in origin. But so, too, is the comfort of the unchallenged soul. Many can rise to the clarion call of a clear challenge. But in our time, the persecution of the faithful may be none other than the relative disinterest many others have in the gospel message. With an unclear enemy and unclear issues, we begin to blend into "sameness." The late William Barclay wrote: "The crisis of the present day is not theological: it is ethical. Christian theology is not really under attack, for there are few outside of the church sufficiently interested in it to assail it."[9]

Gardner C. Taylor comments further: "It is astonishing how much an American family will spend on physical fitness and how little time or interest or money it will invest in spiritual fitness. It is amazing how much attention parents will give to a balanced diet for a child's physical growth and how little attention they will pay to the child's moral and spiritual growth. Bread for the body, but no food for the soul. Cultivation of the mind, none of the heart!"[10]

People in most of our congregations know little of persecution as the early church experienced it. Our homeland has been spared the marching armies for a century and a half, and ours is not a government hostile to our free worship. But the persecution of the church by indifference both within and without the body may well be far more effective than anything in the first century, and ultimately more fearful than either the legions in Palestine or the lions in the Coliseum of Rome.

Jesus' answer is as relevant today as it was to the first-century church: "This will be a time for you to bear testimony." The issue is not "when?" The call is to be faithful in the meantime.

---

1. Kathleen and Leen Ritmeyer, "Reconstructing Herod's Temple Mount in Jerusalem," *Biblical Archaeology Review,* Vol. XV, No. 6, (Washington, D.C., November-December, 1989), p. 26. The quotation of Josephus is from *The Jewish Wars*, Book V, Chapter V.

2. Murray Stein, "How Herod Moved Gigantic Blocks to Construct the Temple Mount," *Biblical Archaeology Review,* Vol. VIII, No. 3, (Washington, D.C., May-June, 1981), p. 42.

3. Benjamin Mazar, "Excavations of the Temple Mount Reveal Splendors of Herodian Jerusalem, *Biblical Archaeology Review,* Vol. VI, No. 4, (Washington, D.C., July-August, 1980), pp. 45-46.

4. *Ibid.*

5. *Ibid.*

6. Andre Parrot, *The Temple of Jerusalem,* (London SCM, Press Ltd., 1957), p. 86.

7. John W. Doberstein, "Introduction," *Life Together,* Dietrich Bonhoeffer, John W. Doberstein, translator, (New York, Harper and Row, Publishers, 1954), p. 18.

8. "The Affirmation of Baptism," *The Lutheran Book of Worship,* (Minneapolis, Augsburg/Fortress Publishing House, 1978), p. 199.

9. William Barclay, *The Ten Commandments for Today,* (New York, Harper and Row, Publishers, 1974), p. 9.

10. Gardner C. Taylor, "Homiletical Interpretation," *Proclamation 2,* Pentecost 3, Series C, Elizabeth Achtemeier, Gerhard Krodel, and Charles P. Price, editors, (Philadelphia, Fortress Press, 1980), p. 57.

A Good Thing To Know

This is one of those times when our gospel lesson tells us too little! To understand today's parable we must first understand the reference to "these things." Events previously reported are the important antecedents to today's reading. "As they heard these things, he [Jesus] proceeded to tell a parable." Luke assumes that his readers know what "things" they (and Jesus' original audience) have been hearing. As we hear the lesson read, we have little chance of knowing. Few are likely to remember that "these things" refers to the story of the conversion of Zacchaeus, a text that we studied five weeks ago![1]

Just What Are "These Things?"

It must have seemed to the disciples that Jesus' popularity with the crowds and the powers of conversion would converge in this mission to Jerusalem and would bring the kingdom's prompt arrival. It was as if Jesus was "on a roll." Finally, things were coming together. Very soon they would be in Jerusalem!

Jesus seizes the moment. He "strikes while the iron is hot," while they were hearing and watching. The things they were hearing, and no doubt were pondering, are several. Each one had its impact. There is the calling of Zacchaeus from the tree. How did Jesus know this was the very right time, the "kairos" for Zacchaeus? There is the conversion of Zacchaeus, no small wonder in itself, given the fact that he was a tax collector, a collaborator with the foreign government of Rome. There were the immediate and sacrificial "fruits" of that conversion. "Behold, Lord, the half of my goods I give to the poor; and if I have defrauded any one of anything, I restore it fourfold (Luke 19:8b-9)." There is the announcement that salvation

95

has come to this publican's house. The definitive declaration that follows is rooted in the shepherd images of Ezekiel: "For the Son of Man came to seek and to save the lost (Luke 19:10)."

Knowing their thoughts, Jesus claims the moment. He presents a parable reinforcing the events of Zacchaeus' house, and he places them into the context of what will be happening in Jerusalem. It will not be what they are expecting. The responses of Zacchaeus will have increased meaning as the disciples begin to struggle with the kingdom of God that is and that is not yet. The fruits of conversion, the style of the redeemed life, and the responsible use of God's gifts here and now will demonstrate that the kingdom is already in our midst through the ministry of the redeemed. God's power is already at work changing lives . . . now! And in the return of Christ, the kingdom is yet to come.

A Blend Of Two Stories

In the parable before us there are two stories, a parable within a parable. The first is from first-century history and is an event well known to virtually everyone. Most would see quickly the parallels and associations.

When Herod the Great died in 4 B.C.E., his son Archelaus went to Rome to have his succession to his father and his kingship confirmed. Though the Romans avoided the use of the title "Rex" for themselves, they did allow the use of the term in some ethnic eastern provinces. Mark Anthony, under senate authority, had given the title to Herod in 40 B.C.E. Through a codicil in Herod's will, Archelaus, as the eldest son, inherited one-half of the kingdom, including Judea, Samaria and Idumea. Now from Rome he sought affirmation and a similar senatorial act. An envoy of 50 Palestinians, Jews and Samaritans were sent to oppose the appointment and to urge autonomy. Others went, too, including Antipater, a stepbrother of Archelaus, who claimed rights to the kingship, along with delegations representing both brothers' claims. After much consideration, Augustus finally awarded to Archelaus the title of "Ethnarch," something less than he had petitioned.

While there is no evidence of a "bloodbath of enemies" upon Archelaus' return, he did inherit something of his father's tendency to such things, as was hinted in the hearings before Augustus. So, when the story tells of a "nobleman who went to a far country to receive a kingdom," there were surely some interesting "flashbacks." Further, we can be sure that Archelaus did not leave Palestine for Rome without leaving trusted servants in charge of the kingdom. From these servants he would ask a full accounting of their management — and their loyalty — during his absence. They were being "tested" even while they "managed."

That's the way life was in those days, and the people knew it. The parable was living and vibrant to its first-century audiences.

All of this brings us to the second story in our parable. That it was a "test" and not the full "management" of a kingdom is clear from the amounts given to each of the three servants specifically mentioned. In Matthew's apparent parallel, a "talent" is given, worth about six times that of a "pound." A "pound" in today's currency is about $25, not a generous amount for the serious management of the king's realm. Though the amount entrusted to each was small — and incidentally, equal — the instructions were, "Trade with these until I come." It was more like a "hands-on civil service exam." Given the small size of the amount entrusted, the servants must have understood this from the beginning. Skill, courage and loyalty to the king and his business are to be measured in the king's absence. From the results of this test the king would build his managerial team. "Well done, good servant! Because you have been faithful in a very little, you shall have authority over ten cities." And to the one who had increased the investment fivefold, he said: "And you are to be over five cities."

This is a story virtually everyone could understand. It is the story of a rather ruthless king returning and immediately testing the loyalties of his staff and perhaps, building his cabinet of assistants. It becomes a powerful sermon illustration built upon the faithfulness of Zacchaeus and the events that begin to unfold in Jerusalem.

But What Does The Story Mean?

The story is clear. But what did Jesus expect his hearers to understand from the parable, and how did it relate to the things seen and heard while visiting with Zacchaeus? What did the Jews hear? What did the disciples hear? Why did Luke tell the story? And finally, what value do all these things have for us, 20 centuries later?

There is an immediate inclination to make the story a simple allegory. Jesus could be the "nobleman" and his journey to the "far country" could be a reference to the coming days in the tomb or the ascension and the return of glory. But Jesus could not be defined as the servant describes the returning king: "I was afraid of you, because you are a severe man; you take up what you did not lay down, and reap what you did not sow." Herod's Archelaus, definitely! Our Father's Christ, definitely not! There are intentional parallels here, but this parable is not an allegory. The sermon illustration must begin for us, "It is as if . . ."

The second story, the one about the faithfulness of the servants, narrows our focus to the third of the servants who reports to the king. At issue are the skill, the courage, the loyalty, the love and the respect of the servant for his king. But this third servant has no kind thing to say for the king — or to him, for that matter — when he returns!

He is judged by the king to be "wicked" because he has disobeyed the king's instructions to "trade" or "do business" with the money entrusted. Even a conservative, acting out of overwrought caution, would have put the money in a bank for the minimal interest of a passbook savings account. More penetrating yet, the king sees something else. By his failure to protect himself with a minimal savings account for the king — just in case the king is the kind of man that he believes him to be — he would appear to have given very little thought to the project in the first place. The king rightly says, "You are trapped by your own words!" It was not alone a matter of caution. He had been slothful and disobedient. At the very least, he had been relatively disinterested.

And now we come to the fulcrum of the parable, the "central luminous truth," upon which hangs the beginning and the ending of our parable. The issue before us is this: How well have we done business with the resources and gifts of the kingdom that have been entrusted to us? It was the question of the first century and it is the question we also must ask of ourselves today.

Suddenly Zacchaeus is in the center of the picture again. He is a faithful servant, an example of how one responds to and uses the gifts of salvation. Instantly, he begins trading and doing business with the gift God has given. "Behold, Lord, the half of my goods I give to the poor; and if I have defrauded any one of anything, I restore it fourfold." With God's gifts come obligations.

Instantly, there were implications for the Jews, the people of promise. For centuries they had been the beneficiaries of God's manifold gifts, but they had done little "trade" with them. There's no question that God's will in these things was clear. God's mighty acts for the rescue of his people were intended to enable their priesthood to the world. How else is one to hear Isaiah as the return from exile is predicted? God does not do these mighty acts in dark corners. They are for all to see. "And the glory of the Lord shall be revealed, and all flesh shall see it together, for the mouth of the Lord has spoken (Isaiah 40:5)."

Seldom were the gifts more obviously hoarded, bound in handkerchiefs and buried in the ground, than in the Old Testament's story of Jonah. For most, the story never moves beyond a curious parable about a whale with indigestion. Instead, it has to do with Israel's need to do God's business with the gifts of its priesthood. It was a difficult lesson for a reluctant Jonah who had no will whatsoever to share the God of Israel with Israel's arch enemy. Further, he found no joy at all when the enemy repented! This refusal to invest the gifts in the work of the kingdom caused many in the New Testament church to believe that the mission, if not the gifts, was taken from the Jews and given to the Gentiles.

The Parable For The Disciples
And First-Century Christians

Earlier it was said that the focus was upon the third servant and that upon this point the beginning and the ending of the parable were affixed as well.

Because the disciples had some reason to believe that the kingdom would come upon their arrival in Jerusalem, Jesus now prepares his disciples to understand the role they are about to assume in God's plan for salvation. After Jesus' ascension, the message will be clearer still to the disciples. They will remember this parable.

The "king" will go into the far country and be there for a while. The kingdom's management will be left in their hands. Soon they will be entrusted with the secrets of the kingdom. Paul, decades later, will write eloquently to the Christians at Corinth: "We have this treasure in earthen vessels, to show that the transcendent power belongs to God and not to us." Though the king appears to be "gone for a while," the kingdom remains the king's kingdom. The disciples and early Christians were the managers left to tend and to trade the resources of the kingdom, not for their own comfort, pleasure and purpose, but for the king's. When the king returns, as he surely will, there will be a day of reckoning!

For the disciples and the early church, Jesus' parable addressed the delay in his return. It encouraged the church to be faithful, doing business with them for the purposes of the kingdom. Productivity in the interim, until the king returned, was — and is — Jesus' powerful point in this parable. This period of the church's life would be a time for brisk kingdom business, to use the word of the nobleman in this parable.

The Parable For Our Times

This message is no less urgent in our times. Living as we do near the close of the second milennium since the ascension, there is no easy way to lay hold of the New Testament urgency in the faithful commerce of the kingdom.

Moreover, the church is increasingly fettered by secular understandings and values that devalue institutions, champion individual freedom over responsibility, and simultaneously urge that religion is a private and personal matter. If we find ourselves busy at all, it is frequently with the wrong things. We think of the church with the same "consumer" mentality that governs our affluent lives. We think of the Christian faith in terms of what we get from it, of what it can do for us, and not of what we can do for our Lord and his church.

Years ago on the mantel at "Nanna Schneider's" house there was a small carving of three monkeys on a fence. My grandmother enjoyed sharing with her young grandson the folk wisdom of the monkeys. It sounded responsible. It was impressive to a youngster still not in kindergarten. One of the monkeys covered his eyes to see no evil. One covered his ears to hear no evil. The third covered his mouth to speak no evil. They were keeping themselves busy staying out of trouble.

Some years later a fuller truth dawned. This "monkey theology" was not nearly responsible enough for Christian discipleship or for a witnessing church. Far too many contemporary Christians understand the goal of their religious life to be that of staying out of trouble — not making any and not causing any! They look quite busy tending the personal treasures of piety, an actively falling far short of "doing business" with the things of the gospel.

101

Looking cautious, caring and busy is not enough. We need to be about the work of the kingdom. Our congregational and personal spiritual lives can never center in our own persons or institutions. We must be busy with evangelism, carrying the good news of Christ, or we are not being faithful.

The Rev. Dr. Gerhard Krodel, Dean of the Lutheran Theological Seminary at Gettysburg, has said:

> *Whenever the Church is in trouble, it does three things. It fiddles with the structure. It raises new moneys, and it changes the liturgy. It gives the impression of being very busy when in truth, it is not. The church in Germany during the 1930s did all three, looking very busy. In truth, it should have been busy opposing the rise of anti-Semitism.*[2]

And It's A Good Thing To Know

More often than not, one has just a touch of sympathy for the servant who, intimidated by the king, buries the pound. "Wicked" seems a harsh judgment. At least he did not lose it!

Closer examination brings us to see that the servant has disobeyed the king. He has not followed instructions. He has shown little care or even thoughtful caution. Had he worried as much as he said, he would at least have covered himself with a minimum usefulness. His mind had not been much on the king or on the king's business. Isn't it so!

So, too, it seems to be with many who accept the title of "Christian." They have little intention of becoming disciples. Therefore, there are important lessons to be learned here.

1. Everyone is gifted in the kingdom. Paul writes: "to each is given the manifestation of the spirit for the common good." At baptism, each of us becomes a servant of the king, and we are given gifts with which to do the business of the kingdom.

2. Our gifts are to be invested in the kingdom. Again, Paul writes to the Christians at Ephesus that our gifts are for "the building up of the body of Christ." They are not alone for

our spiritual security or our pride. Each of us is a part of the body of Christ. Regardless of the apparent importance of each of our functions in that body, each part is necessary for the good health and function of all of its parts.

3. Each one received the same amount, but they were not equally skillful in its investment. Similarly, God gives each of us gifts that are equally useful for our salvation and for the work of the kingdom. We are measured not by our success, but by our faithfulness and our obedience.

4. There are, therefore, no secret saints. We are entrusted with the management of the kingdom until the king returns. The Christian faith and life are not personal things "kept within our hearts." Christians do not hide their light under a bushel. Salvation shows, just as it did for Zacchaeus. Christians living in the light and power of the gospel are expected to bring the experience of the kingdom into the midst of the world and into the experience of others. In that sense, the kingdom is already in our midst, even though we await the return of our king to claim his kingdom.

5. There will come a day of reckoning when we must report to the king how faithfully we have done his business with the gifts he has given us.

No wonder then, that Paul counsels the Corinthians to be "steadfast, immovable, always abounding in the work of the Lord, knowing that in the Lord your labor is not in vain."

Now there's good news! The spontaneous stewardship of a Zacchaeus, the determined and self-sacrificing work of a missionary, and our own day-by-day trade in our gifts for the things of the kingdom are important parts of the architecture of God's plan for our salvation. Not a single "transaction" is lost. Our labor in behalf of the king, until he returns, is not ever in vain. Our work is worthwhile. It makes a difference, which is to say in another way, "We make a difference." And that's good news!

It's a good thing to know.

Amen.

1. Luke 19:1-10. This is the gospel appointed for Proper 26, Ordinary Time 31, Pentecost 24.

2. The Rev. Dr. Gerhard Krodel, who retired in 1991 as dean of the Lutheran Theological Seminary at Gettysburg, Pennsylvania. Dr. Krodel has given permission for the use of this quotation from an unpublished lecture.

At The Name Of Jesus

It was the season of the Passover, one of the three feasts of obligation for the faithful Jews of the first century. Jerusalem overflowed with religious pilgrims — people who by their very definition took the things of faith seriously. Some authorities estimate that there could have been as many as 2,700,000. In one such Passover season, it was reported that 256,500 lambs were sacrificed, about one for each 10 pilgrims.[1] The mood was one of religious fervor and of celebration.

On this particular day, the air around Jerusalem bristled with a new excitement. Never before had anyone dead for four days been called from the grave. In an instant, Lazarus had become a celebrity among the pilgrims. Jesus' name was on everyone's lips.

Spontaneously the crowds began to gather at Bethany, not alone to see Jesus, but especially to see Lazarus, to confirm for themselves that it was true — that it could be believed. The dead can live again! The little town of Bethany must have been inundated with the crowds of the curious and the hopeful.

Hosanna! Long Live The King

The dawn of the next day brought new excitement. People heard that Jesus was coming to Jerusalem, to the Holy City itself. Now a great new crowd surged out of the city to meet him. The crowds of the disciples, the folks that had the day before gone to Bethany, and the people coming out of the city converged and flowed together like the tides.

Those coming from the city brought palms, a familiar tradition for a day of celebration. They had carried palms on the day that Judas Macccabaeus rededicated the temple following the rule of the Syrians. They carried them on the Feast of the Tabernacles. Spontaneously the chant began; "Hosanna! Blessed is he who comes in the name of the Lord, even the King of Israel!" To shout "Hosanna" was on the one hand not unlike the modern-day "God save the King!" in spirit, and on the other hand a plea for help and deliverance. It means, "Save us!"

As the crowd swirled and the chants became more rhythmical, Jesus found a young ass, and immediately climbed upon the animal, to ride it into the city. The crowd must have cheered all the more at this intentional fulfillment of the prophecy of Zephaniah: "Behold, your king is coming, sitting on an ass' colt." Jesus has affirmed the title of king, and by his conscious act he affirms this moment as the time of the king's arrival. This was surely their day. The king has come, and with him, the kingdom.

The Misunderstood King

Since at least the eighth century B.C.E., the prophets had promised and the people had looked for the coming of an "ideal ruler." The name "messiah" at this stage was a generic one that meant "anointed." Every king of Israel was anointed by God and given authority to rule over God's people. The hunger was for a righteous king of the Davidic line who would lead Israel to worldwide dominion. As Israel's political fortunes worsened, first with the fall of the Northern Kingdom to the Assyrians in the eighth century B.C.E., and later with the fall of Judah and Jerusalem in the sixth century B.C.E. to the Babylonians, and the exile that followed, the hope of the messiah turned toward political independence and vindication.

By the time of Christ, this expectation had become very popular, as the Dead Sea Scrolls have indicated. No longer was "messiah" or "anointed" applied to all Jewish kings.

God's anointed would now be God's very special one who would deliver the pious.

Having heard of the miracles of Jesus, the raising of Lazarus, and even of Jesus' skill in silencing the theological debates of the Sadducees, the pilgrims of that Passover season believed that it was just a matter of time until the trumpets would blare and the call to arms would come and the Jewish people would be swept to a much-hungered-for victory over Rome. So they shouted "Hosanna!" "Save us!"

This was a nationalistic demonstration. Just as the large crowd in Galilee had misunderstood the meaning of the multiplication of the loaves and fishes and had sought to make him a king by force, so the crowd in Jerusalem and Bethany had misunderstood the raising of Lazarus. They sought to put to their own limited uses the "King" who could quiet the seas, offer the bread of life, and raise up the dead.

Though all four gospels report the entry into Jerusalem, there are differences in the order of things. Particularly significant is John's note that Jesus discovers and mounts the donkey after he has heard, and accepted, the acclamation of the crowds. Noting the strong nationalistic emphasis of the cheering crowd, Jesus seeks to "correct" their misunderstanding of his kingship. He accepts the title, but not the program. Ancient eastern kings rode horses when riding to war, and donkeys when they came in peace. It was not the humility of the donkey but the symbol of peace that Jesus sought, even as he accepted the acclaim and the title of "King" by fulfilling Zechariah's prophecy. Jesus intended to be the Prince of Peace and to bring the kingdom of God.

The Two Kingdoms Meet

The interface of these two kingdoms is the crisis of Holy Week and the challenge of every devout Christian life since that day. The charges brought to Pilate are of alleged treasonable acts and teachings, misleading the people and claiming to be a king. Patronizing the Romans to manipulate their desired judgment against the Christ, they affirm their "loyalty" to Caesar. "We have no king but Caesar!" the chief priest shouted. Pilate, who cared little about the religious squabbles of the Jews, understood full well the political implications of the charges. His question to Jesus pressed the point: "Are you the King of the Jews?"

As he had done in the tumultuous procession a few days earlier, Jesus accepted the title of King, though not the terms usually associated with the title. "My kingship is not of this world; if my kingship were of this world, my servants would fight . . . ." "So you are a king?" Pilate answers. Again, Jesus affirms the title: "You say that I am a king; for this I was born and for this I have come into the world, to bear witness to the truth. Everyone who is of the truth hears my voice."

Cynical about "truth" apart from power and authority, Pilate quickly assessed that Jesus was not a serious threat to Rome and sought to release him. A king without either an army or an earthly kingdom was not to be feared, or so he thought.

Apparently the crowd had similar thoughts. A king who refuses a kingdom is not to be respected. Disillusioned and disappointed, the shouts of "Hosanna" soon turned to "Crucify." While Pilate worried only about "real" kings, the crowd had neither respect nor use for anything less.

Citizens Of Christ's Kingdom

While Jesus will later say to Pilate, "My kingship is not of this world," and will say another time similarly, "My kingship is not from this world," the truth is that when Christ comes, the kingdom of God impacts upon our world as surely as a meteor falling from the sky strikes the earth! Systems and ideas, peoples and politics, lifestyles and goals all come under the judgment of the new king. New standards come into place immediately! The powers and works of darkness must no longer be the norm of behavior. Cynical truth, measured by politics, armies, compromise and convenience (as well as justice that works in the same fashion!) are replaced with God's righteous and unchanging truth. Specifically, citizenship in God's kingdom is measured by truth. Jesus says as much: "I have come into the world to bear witness to the truth. Everyone who is of the truth hears my voice." The credentials of citizenship in the kingdom of God are no less than to hear and follow the voice of truth, which is Jesus Christ.

The implications of citizenship in this kingdom are clear. We may not be "of this world," but as the people of God, Christians are clearly in it. That makes the kingdom not a dream of "pie in the sky by and by," but a challenge to live as law-abiding citizens of that kingdom right now.

There are few better lessons of the kingdom's potential impact than those of today's gospel lesson. Responsible, competent and respected religious leaders, focused on priorities other than the truth, placed themselves directly into the path of the coming kingdom. Neither listening to, nor searching to know the truth, they become citizens of the kingdom of darkness, seeking to extinguish the light.

One has little difficulty understanding their panic as John tells us the story. The news of the powerful works of Jesus had caused large defections from the orthodox faith. As Jesus moved toward Jerusalem, the problems of containing the demonstrations and the defections worsened. They believed he was wrong in his teachings, and they worried that he could lead a rebellion against Rome. They knew Rome's hand was hard and swift in such cases. Moderates who thought collaboration with Rome was the wise policy, and men of the priestly family who had wealth, comfort and security had so much to lose. I happen to believe that they were sincere in believing that the nation of Israel had much to lose, too. Responsible leaders must sometimes make difficult decisions.

So they made them. Already they had decided, upon hearing the news of the hundreds that had witnessed Jesus' raising of Lazarus, that the nation was "best served" by putting Jesus to death. Now, upon hearing the news in today's lesson of the crowds that flocked to see Lazarus, they planned to put Lazarus to death also.

Where there should have been celebration, there was despair. The Pharisees said to one another: "You see that you can do nothing; look, the world has gone after him." They were honestly concerned, but they were not listening for the voice of truth. Given the signs, one might suppose that they would have done some careful investigation. He had calmed the sea, fed thousands, healed every sort of disease, opened the eyes of the blind, and raised the dead. At his word the dead heard, the dumb spoke, and the lame walked. Hundreds, sometimes thousands, were witnesses. Frequently they had initiated confrontation with Jesus. Never had they been open to conversation. At least, so it seems!

Rather incredible, isn't it? They abandoned every principle to destroy this one who clearly had powers none could equal. Nothing would be enough until he was dead. Imagine those who awaited the messiah and who hungered for Israel's vindication shouting, "We have no king but Caesar!" William Barclay notes: "A man comes to a sorry pass when he is afraid of the truth and when he sets his personal prestige and profit before the truth.[1]

H. C. Woods tells the story of two women who were reacting to having heard, for the first time, of Charles Darwin's theory of evolution. "Let's hope it's not true; and, if it is, let's hush it up."

Living In The Kingdom

To be a citizen of the kingdom of God, the follower of the Prince of Peace and the voice of truth, one must forever be open to the truth of God, and that truth always impacts with our world, our time, and our lives.

For many, the kingdom is not of this world at all. Spiritualized and intellectualized, it becomes intangible. Believing in Christ does not result in following the Christ. It does not result in real changes of values, priorities and lifestyles. It does not reform our dealings with one another, challenge our politics, or seriously modify our behavior. The kingdom is tomorrow. Today is the "real" world. Leading national magazines now and again chastise the church, urging preachers to keep religion in the pulpit and politics out, even though a reading of today's lesson is first and foremost a story of the confrontation by the very essence of the gospel with the realities of secular politics. The entry into Jerusalem was a demonstration Jesus carefully staged, riding rather intentionally into the teeth of the politics of the secular and religious authorities.

This "spiritualization" of the kingdom, removing its demands from the arena of our world has been an ongoing problem for the church. It becomes a refuge from today's responsibility. In a lecture prepared in 1932 for the last Sunday in the church year, Dietrich Bonhoeffer wrote:

> *Whenever life begins to be oppressive and troublesome, a person just leaps into the air with a bold kick and soars relieved and unencumbered into the so-called eternal fields. He leaps over the present. He disdains the earth . . . . After all, besides the temporal defeats, he has the eternal victories, and they are so easily achieved.*[2]

To live under the kingship of Christ requires a radical change of thinking. We think of power, Jesus thinks of love. We think of security, but Jesus thinks of risk-taking for the gospel. (He talked of "cross bearing.") We ask what we can get from a relationship. Jesus asks what we can give. Jesus calls us to ask, "What can I do in Christ's name for you?" We ask, "What's in it for me?"

Like Paul, we struggle always with the truth about ourselves. "I can will what is right, but I cannot do it. For I do not do the good that I want, but the evil I do not want is what I do (Romans 7:18b-19)." Because of this, we ourselves will never fully bring the kingdom; only Christ will do that when he comes. However, living under Christ the King and struggling to be faithful, we bring the kingdom to the people and places where we are. W. Frank Harrington provides a very real definition of what the challenge of living in the kingdom, under the kingship of Christ, calls us to be:

> The kingdom is based on truth and love, where those who follow would practice love and seek the truth, where needs of neighbor would equal concern for self. A kingdom where cheeks would be turned, where second miles would be walked, where cloaks would be given to cover the nakedness of one who had no cloak, where enemies would be prayed for, not hated, where persecutors would feel the pressure of the Golden Rule, where sharing would be more prevalent than shoving, where hate would give way to love, where caring would overcome indifference, and where truth would be stronger than falsehood.[3]

We have a king. He has a kingdom, and that kingdom is already in our midst. He is the king over all history and over all creation. He is our Lord. Paul, most probably quoting an early Christian incarnational hymn, has written:

> Have this mind among yourselves which you have in Christ Jesus: Who though he was in the form of God, did not regard equality with God as something to be exploited, but emptied himself, taking the form of a servant, being born in the likeness of men. And being found in human form, he humbled himself and became obedient unto death, even death on a cross.
>
> Therefore, God has highly exalted him and bestowed upon him a name that is above every name, that at the name of Jesus, every knee should bow, in heaven and on earth and under the earth, and every tongue confess that Jesus Christ is Lord, to the glory of God the Father. (Philippians 2:5-11).

And the Pharisees said to one another: "You see that you can do nothing; look, the whole world has gone after him." Would that it were already so! Come Lord Jesus!

1. William Barclay, *The Gospel of John,* Vol. 2, (Philadelphia, The Westminster Press, 1956), p. 135.

2. Dietrich Bonhoeffer, "Thy Kingdom Come: The Prayer of the Church for the Kingdom of God on Earth," *A Testament to Freedom: The Essential Writings of Dietrich Bonhoeffer,* Geffrey B. Kelly and F. Burton Nelson, Editors, (San Francisco, HarperCollins Publishers, 1990), p. 94.

3. W. Frank Harrington, *Seeking a Living Faith,* (Lima, C.S.S. Publishing Co., Inc., 1988), p. 84.

The Potentate Of Time

There was a sense of anxiety as our seminary classmates gathered that day. To a person they had been surprised when the professor announced that there would be a final exam. Everyone was asking, "How can you have a final exam in preaching?" How could one prepare? What sort of questions might be asked? Throughout the year there had been lectures on sermon preparation and style, but mostly it had been a course of practice and critique.

Finally, the professor, who was himself a splendid and engaging preacher, strode into the room and a quiet fell. The familiar blue books were distributed.

"Gentlemen," he began, "you may use your Bibles for this exam. You have three hours. There is just one question and it has three parts. Here it is: You have one last sermon to preach in your ministry. It's your last best shot. Choose your text and theme, explain why you have chosen them, and give a full, detailed outline for the development of that sermon." That morning and that question have left lasting marks upon this preacher's life and his ministry!

Christ The King

Today brings us that one last shot in this church year. Today the church brings to conclusion all that has been revealed and celebrated in the gospel story of God's work for our salvation since that story began with Advent's hope a year ago. Today it must come together for us into one concluding proclamation about Jesus Christ who is "King of kings and Lord of lords." And today we must address that ultimate question about Christ's lordship in our lives and in our world.

115

From the beginning of the church's year, we have been hearing about the king who was coming, the anointed one of God who would save his people. Astrologers from the east came inquiring of Herod, "Where is he who has been born king of the Jews?" When called as a disciple, Nathanael answered, almost prophetically, "Rabbi, you are the Son of God! You are the King of Israel." At one point in Jesus' ministry, the people responded so enthusiastically that they were about to come and take him by force to make him king. When Jesus rides into Jerusalem, he purposefully fulfills the prophecy of Zechariah: "Lo, your king comes to you, humble and riding upon a donkey," and the people greet him with the shout: "Blessed is the King who comes in the name of the Lord."

Kingship is the center around which the charges against Jesus are brought to Pilate. "Are you the king of the Jews?" Pilate asks. Hours later, Pilate gives his own sarcastic affirmation in the legally required statement of charges placed on the cross: "This is the King of the Jews." The ridicule of the bystanders and the hope of the penitent thief are bound up in this same kingship in today's gospel lesson. "If you are the King of the Jews, save yourself!" the soldiers taunted. The crowd loved it! The penitent thief cries out: "Jesus, remember me when you come into your kingly power." In the title of "king" there is the occasion of ridicule and the opportunity of hope. It was so then. It seems equally so now.

In the good news of the resurrection, we have celebrated the victory of Christ over death and the powers of evil. Throughout the Pentecost season we have studied the kingdom of God and what it means to live in that kingdom in the light of the resurrection of Christ. Christ is the lord of our lives. Christ is the king.

Suddenly the old professor's question is our question. To what lesson do we turn? What theme do we select to pull together into one proclamation and celebration all that we have heard and seen about our Christ? This should be a day of prophetic hope and of a clear christological statment of the Incarnation, a day of important last words. "If you had one last sermon to preach, what would it be?"

Christ, The Power And The Wisdom Of God

With such thoughts in mind, today's gospel lesson comes as a surprise, if not as an outright shock. God's anointed king is dying like a common criminal. To a casual observer on that early Friday afternoon, things were not going all that well for the "king." Though there had been moments of huge crowd support, times when a voice spoke from heaven, and hopes that the kingdom of God was dawning with power at any moment, today's lesson hardly gives that impression. It seems as if some committee chose the lesson because the word "king" is used frequently. How can one look at the cross and call it a throne? How can we see the defeat of death and proclaim it a victory? Surely there must be a better text for our last sermon of the year. Isn't it so!

Then again, maybe not! It was Paul who wrote to the Christians at Corinth that he had resolved to know nothing except Jesus Christ and him crucified. Earlier Paul noted with candor that such preaching was "a stumbling block to Jews and folly to Gentiles, but to those who are called . . . [it is] Christ the power of God and the wisdom of God."

Though Luke reports the crucifixion in just 14 verses, it became for the early church the center of its preaching. Luke demonstrates this well in the preaching he records in the Book of the Acts of the Apostles. There is here virtually all we need to know about the grace and the forgiveness of God, just as Paul has suggested.

Crown Him The Lord Of Love

Throughout the "Year of Luke" in our lectionary series we have heard Luke's favorite theme. The ready and generous grace of God is shown repeatedly. In recent Sundays we studied the story of the healing of 10 lepers, an act of God's love and grace. We have watched as Jesus, like the promised shepherd of Ezekiel, came searching for the lost and hiding

Zacchaeus. We have overheard the prayers of the Pharisee and the Publican as they prayed in Jesus' parable, all the while being reminded of our need to trust God's grace. None of us can forget Jesus' words just before the beginning of today's lesson: "Father, forgive them, for they know not what they do." The ever-present grace of God is one of Luke's gospel themes.

From the parables of the waiting father and the "good" Samaritan, and now from the story of the penitent thief on the cross, all of these reported only by Luke, we have heard forthrightly the good news of Jesus Christ. Gentile and Jew, sinner and saint, young and old, it makes no difference. The full blessings of forgiveness here and hereafter are available to all who repent. The love of God reaches out for all, even to those who would arrange the crucifixion and taunt its victim. "Father, forgive them . . . ."

Nor is there a time too late! From the parable of the laborers in the vineyard to the real-life moment of the thief on the cross, God's grace prevails, even to the last hour, even to the last moment. "Jesus, remember me when you come into your kingdom." The response is swift and direct. "Truly, I say to you, today you will be with me in Paradise."

In this exchange, Luke reaches the peak of his report of the crucifixion, the manifestation of God's "salvific mercy to one of the dregs of humanity."[1]

Frederick William Faber grasped the moment for us as he penned the lines of his popular hymn:

> There is welcome for the sinner,
>   And a promised grace made good;
> There is mercy with the savior;
>   There is healing in his blood.[2]

On this Friday afternoon, it was "last sermon" time. It was the moment of truth for both Jesus and the criminal who repented. Jesus had preached the grace of God creatively and powerfully. The thief, in his repentance, calls upon Jesus to make those promises good. And he does. Clearly, the love of God is broader than the measures of our mind. Paul writes:

> *In all these things we are more than conquerors through him who loved us. For I am sure that neither death, nor life, nor angels, nor principalities, nor things present, nor things to come, nor powers, nor height, nor depth, nor anything else in all creation, will be able to separate us from the love of God in Christ Jesus, our Lord (Romans 8:37-39).*

Jesus Christ is our Lord. Jesus Christ is our king. Crown him with many crowns! Crown him the Lord of Love!''

Crown Him The Lord Of Life

Today's lesson carries us beyond its moment and into a new age of history — an age yet to come. In a single sentence from the crucified Christ, the finite is merged with the infinite, the here is joined to the hereafter, the now is joined to what has been until now the ''not yet.'' All that has come before is joined to all that is promised to come. He does it with a single phrase, ''Today, you will be with me in Paradise.''

Jesus Christ is king in this age and the next, in this world and the next. There seems to be a willingness for many to accept the teachings of Jesus but not the divinity of the Christ. Many cannot accept the eternal dimensions that come most naturally with Christ and his teachings. Today's gospel brings us squarely before Jesus' claim.

The criminal, having admitted his own guilt, acknowledges Jesus' kingly state by his request. He begs to be remembered in whatever future awaits them. By his asking, he is begging a gift only a king over the next life has any authority to give.

From our side of the resurrection, it is easy to miss the fact that only Luke, among all the evangelists, presents the destiny of Christ as a part of the crucifixion narrative. Here Christ will transcend life and the death with which this life ends. Beyond this, the details are not clear.

119

This is not to say that paradise is without meaning. It is a word of Persian origin, and it refers to a garden. The late Dr. William Barclay writes that it was a walled garden.[3] When a Persian king wanted to do a favor for a subject, he invited that person to walk with him in the garden. Jesus was promising the penitent thief more than immortality, and certainly more than the "dwelling in the shadows of the neither here nor there" of some of the contemporary theories and mythologies. He promised him the gift of companionship, of walking with him in the courts of heaven.

Though Luke is the only one to report for us this moment of repentance and salvation during the hours of the crucifixion, this story is fully consistent with the witness of the other evangelists and the writers of the epistles. In John's gospel the "walled garden" becomes "my Father's house" of "many rooms," to which Jesus is going to prepare a place for us. Paul comforts the troubled Christians at Thessalonica with the assurance that the dead in Christ will be raised first, and "then we who are alive shall be caught up together with them in the clouds to meet the Lord in the air; and so shall we always be with the Lord." Whether we speak of a walled garden, a house of many rooms, or being gathered together in the clouds, it matters not! The important words are these: "Today you will be with me . . . ."

Christ is the king who speaks with authority not alone about the grace of God in this life, but about the destiny of this life as well. This destiny is not a "perk" for contemporary piety. It is such a substantial part of the good news that Paul has written: "If for this life only we have hope in Christ, we are of all men most to be pitied. (1 Corinthians 15:19)."

> *Crown him the Lord of Life,*
> *Who triumphed o'er the grave*
> *And rose victorious in the strife*
> *For those he came to save.*[4]

Crown Him The Lord Of Years,
The Potentate Of Time

Jesus Christ is King. He is the Lord of our lives in this world and the next. He is Lord of lords and King of kings. He is the lord of all creation.

This cosmic kingship, spanning all time and space, is proclaimed eloquently by the epistle to the Colossians. "He [Christ] is before all things, and in him all things hold together . . . For in him all the fullness of God was pleased to dwell, and through him to reconcile to himself all things, whether on earth or in heaven, making peace by the blood of Christ (Colossians 1:17, 19-20)."

The echoes of this cosmic authority and presence are heard throughout the New Testament. John begins his gospel with the profound words of his prologue: "In the beginning was the Word, and the Word was with God, and the Word was God; all things were made through him, and without him was not anything made that was made . . . And the Word became flesh and dwelt among us, full of grace and truth (John 1:1-3, 14)."

Later in the same gospel, Jesus proclaims: "Before Abraham was, I am!" In the Transfiguration, reported by Matthew, Mark, and Luke, Jesus discusses with Moses and Elijah his departure which he is to accomplish in Jerusalem. Moses the law-giver and Elijah the ancient prophet remain part of the "team" working for our redemption. Jesus Christ is the Lord of history and of eternity. He is the lord of time and of space. He is the "Potentate of Time."

Extending The King's Rule

The excitement of the early church can be explained only in part by the good news of redemption and the lively hope of resurrection to life everlasting. They had been commissioned to go into all the world, make disciples of all nations and to extend the rule of the king and the blessings of the kingdom.

Theirs was a grateful response that struggled with urgency to tell the good news and to spread the kingdom. That restless urgency is caught up in Paul's words to the Colossians. "It is he whom we proclaim, warning everyone and teaching everyone in all wisdom, so that we may present everyone mature in Christ. For this I toil and struggle with all the energy that he powerfully inspires within me (Colossians 1:28-29)."

Christ's victory over the powers of evil is assured. His victory over death is won. His place in eternity has been from the beginning. He is King of all kings. He is Lord of all lords.

Still, there are places where he does not yet rule. He is Lord of lords, but is he the Lord of our lives? On this last Sunday of the church year we have told the story yet another time. And another time, Christ awaits our response.

Is Christ the Lord of our lives, the Lord of our time, and the Lord of our use of our wealth and our skills? Is he the "King" in whose service we daily rejoice? Are we faithful stewards of the properties of the kingdom to which we have been entrusted? We know he rules the heavens. But does he rule our hearts?

Alexander McClaren has observed that on Calvary there were two thieves crucified with Jesus. One thief was saved [so] that no man need despair, but only one, [so] that no man might presume.[5]

It's the last Sunday of the church year. If there were one last sermon to preach, one last time to tell the story, what would you choose? Or better still, what will the answer be when the story ends? The king waits.

> Crown him with many crowns,
>   The Lamb upon his throne;
> Hark how the heavenly anthem drowns
>   All music but its own.
> Awake, my soul, and sing
>   Of him who died for thee,
> And hail him as thy matchless king
>   Through all eternity.[6]

1. Joseph A. Fitzmyer, S.J., *The Gospel According to Luke X-XXIV,* The Anchor Bible, Vol. 28, (Garden City, Doubleday and Company, Inc., 1985), p. 1508.

2. Frederick William Faber, "There's a Wideness in God's Mercy," *Lutheran Book of Worship, op. cit.* Hymn 290, Stanza 2.

3. William Barclay, *The Gospel of Luke,* (Philadelphia, The Westminster Press, 1956), p. 299.

4.. Matthew Bridges, "Crown Him with Many Crowns," *Lutheran Book of Worship,* Hymn 170, excerpted from Stanza 4, (Minneapolis, Augsburg Publishing House, 1978).

5. O. C. Edwards, Jr. and Gardner C. Taylor, *Proclamation 2,* Pentecost 3, Series C, (Philadelphia, Fortress Press, 1980), p. 64.

6. Matthew Bridges, op. cit., Stanza 1.

The Spontaneous Routine

The Duty Of A Nation

History records that the Pilgrims celebrated a good harvest as early as 1621, and that Massachusetts celebrated a thanksgiving day now and again until the 18th century. But our first President, George Washington, is credited with establishing our first national day of prayer and thanksgiving. By proclamation President George Washington set aside November 26, 1790, as a day of official thanksgiving "for the many single favors of Almighty God."

In that first proclamation, President Washington wrote:

It is the duty of all nations to acknowledge the providence of Almighty God, to obey his will, to be grateful for his benefits, and humbly to implore his protection and power . . .[1]

A request by President Washington that the Congress establish an annual observance of such a day was ignored. The next national day of thanksgiving would be by the proclamation of President Abraham Lincoln. He, too, would write about the duty of gratitude.

It is the duty of nations as well as of men to own their dependence upon the overruling power of God, to confess their sins and transgressions in humble sorrow, yet with assured hope that genuine repentance will lead to mercy and pardon.[2]

Writing in the midst of the Civil War, the president understandably calls for a national day of prayer for repentance of sins and transgressions and for prayers for mercy and pardon. More often than not, humility and thanksgiving were mingled in those days, giving us something of a "Day of Thanksgiving" and a "Day of Atonement" as well.

It has become a tradition for our presidents to call us to the "duty of gratitude," even suggesting that thanksgiving is "our joyous duty." Surely there is worth in such things. Calling upon our nation to set apart a day for prayer, for centering our thoughts and values within our several religious traditions, promises blessings not unlike the Old Testament's sabbath of rest and remembrance.

Nevertheless, and with no unkind criticism intended, the call to the "duty of gratitude" leaves us rather "cold." Duty can produce an obedient people, but it is not likely to produce a grateful people. Thanksgiving is what we want to be about on this day. But who knows what thanksgiving is about?

Biblically speaking, thanksgiving is the outpouring of gratitude in response to God's mighty acts and the motivation of the religious life. Gratitude has at least three important qualities. Gratitude is spontaneous. Gratitude is as specific as the moment and as generic as a lifestyle. And finally, gratitude is a gift of the Spirit.

Gratitude Is Spontaneous

Though our presidents speak of the "duty of gratitude," the grateful heart cannot be commanded, cajoled, or manipulated. For some, the smallest gesture brings an outflow of appreciation. For others, the hugest of all gifts can go unacknowledged.

There's hardly a better example than the gospel lesson appointed for this day: "On the way to Jerusalem, he was passing along between Samaria and Galilee. And as he entered a village, he was met by ten lepers, who stood at a distance and lifted up their voices and said, "Jesus, Master, have mercy on us (Luke 17:11-13)!"

126

Always the master storyteller, Luke wastes not a word as he introduces our story. "Standing at a distance," indeed! That was the plight of everyone certified by the priests as a "leper." When the wind was blowing from the leper toward a healthy person, it was prescribed that they must stand 50 yards in the distance. Removed to "reservations" in valleys and gorges outside of the towns, they were kept far from family and friends. Food was carried and left a safe distance from the colony, a neutral area, to which the members of the colony would then come. When it was necessary to go into the town, the leper would shout, "Unclean! Unclean!" Some carried a little bell. Its tinkling sound very nearly mimicked the terrible word: "Ding-a-ling!" "Unclean!"

"Unclean!" The alienation and loneliness were as pressing a burden as the disease. In ancient Hebrew tradition, "unclean" was a ceremonial term, not a medical one. To be a leper was to be "unclean" before God as well. Though not considered a sin in itself, leprosy was viewed as an act of God. Priests were required to identify both the curse of the disease and the miracle of its cure. The book of Deuteronomy gives precise instructions. Healing was invariably interpreted as a miracle of God. To be a leper was to live as if under the judgment of God on the one hand, and outside of the grace of God on the other.

No wonder, then, that they cried, "Jesus, Master, have mercy on us!" Mercy and grace were the only sources of hope for healing the disease, ending the alienation from God and providing restoration to the fellowship of family and friends.

Luke continues the story: Jesus commands the 10 to go and show themselves to the priests. Obeying Jesus, they went, and during the journey they were healed. If ever there were candidates for spontaneous gratitude, they must surely be these 10 newly-cleansed people.

It may be assumed that nine continued on their journey to the priests for the verification of the healing. But one of the 10, overwhelmed by the miracle of grace he has received, momentarily abandons the journey to the priests and returns "praising God with a loud voice," and "he fell at Jesus' feet, giving him thanks." Luke's next words add to the impact of the apparent ingratitude of the others. "Now he was a Samaritan."

Gratitude is spontaneous. It cannot be manipulated or cajoled. It cannot, apparently, be purchased. Today's gospel rightfully casts serious doubt on the validity of the oft-given counsel, "Count your blessings!" One of the greatest blessings God can give, the healing of leprosy, does not guarantee either a grateful heart or an act of thanksgiving. The rivers of our gratitude are fed from the wells of a deeper source.

Gratitude Is A Routine, A Lifestyle

Albert Schweitzer, writing about the 10 lepers, surmises that "all·the 10, surely, were grateful, but none of them hurried home first . . . One of them, however, had a disposition which made him act at once as his feelings bade him; he sought out the person who had helped him and refreshed his soul with the spirit of gratitude."[3]

A "disposition" to act spontaneously on one's feelings suggests that gratitude is for that person a "natural response," unplanned and unreasoned, and flowing out of a pattern of life that makes an act of gratitude as specific as the cause of the moment and as generic as a lifestyle.

Paul counsels Timothy that "supplications, prayers, intercessions and thanksgivings be made for everyone." In every epistle that is recognized as authentically "Pauline" (except the Epistle to the Galatians), Paul begins with a fully developed expression of thanksgiving, calling into memory the way God's Spirit has worked among that particular gathering of Christians. In Philippians 4:5, Paul urges that if one is making a request of God, let it be done with thanksgiving. In Colossians, watchful prayer is offered with thanksgiving, and speech is always to be gracious. On another occasion, Paul urges us to "rejoice always, pray constantly, [and] give thanks in all circumstances.

"All circumstances" means that gratitude is the quality of our lives in both the good times and the bad. Though the providence of God is a major ingredient in the thankful life, it is not a matter of "counting blessings" as a cause for thanksgiving. We are urged to give thanks in all circumstances. It is a lifestyle, a spontaneous routine, as specific as the cause of the moment and as generic as a lifestyle. It flourishes in all times and in all circumstances.

Gratitude Is A Gift Of The Spirit

Gratitude, celebrated in a moment, is always more than that moment alone. It becomes the motivation of the Christian life centered upon one's experience of and dependence upon the security of God's providential care. The secure spirit faces the challenges and dangers of life in the assurance of God's participating presence, so that there develops a "peace which this world cannot give," that "being defended from the fear of our enemies," we may "pass our time in rest and quietness." God is, after all, the one "from whom all holy desires, all good councils, and all just works do proceed."

The biblical mandates and exhortations direct us to remember God's mighty acts for our salvation. Our blessings are counted neither to horde the largess of God's blessings nor to make us grateful because we have more than God seems to have given another. Such actions play to our greed, our competitiveness, and to the erosion of our faith. (How many blessings . . . or how much grace . . . is ever enough?)

Rather, seeing the patterns of God's grace, his unswerving faithfulness, and his steady work for our salvation, we have faith in his continuing ability and desire to provide for our needs. "We know that in everything God works for the good with those who love him." It is the confidence in God's providential presence, not the balance sheet of our accumulated blessings, that forms and feeds the root of gratitude.

Moreover, gratitude and commitment go "hand in hand." Gratitude leads to acts of thanksgiving — the first thought and the first response — and thanksgiving leads to submission to God's will. None of us can fail to recall the stirring story of the day Isaiah "went to church." Suddenly he was confronted with the presence of God and he feared for his life. "I am a man of unclean lips and I dwell among a people of unclean lips, and I shall surely die!" An angel touches his lips with a hot coal from the altar, and Isaiah hears the words, "you are clean!" Isaiah is elated! Then he overhears the conversations of God, "Who will go for us? Whom can we send?" In thanksgiving and overwhelming gratitude, Isaiah cries out, "Here I am! Send me!"

Gratitude, born in the quiet and confident soul, is a fruit of faith, and faith is God's gift. Luther, remembering Jesus' exclamation at Caesarea Philippi, writes:

> *I believe that by my own reason or strength I cannot believe in Jesus Christ, my Lord, or come to him. But the Holy Spirit has called me through the Gospel, enlightened me with his gifts, and sanctified and preserved me in true faith, just as he calls, gathers, enlightens and sanctifies the whole Christian church on earth . . . .*[4]

A Last Question

For those who have come today to worship, heeding our president's call to the "duty of giving thanks," one question remains.

Clearly, not all the blessed are thankful. For some, even the healing of 10 lepers seems too little to strike a joyous chord of thanksgiving or even a word of appreciation. There are others who are gracious even in difficult times. Still others can be surly and demanding in the best of circumstances.

But it seems clear that gratitude and the expressions of thanksgiving have three common qualities: They are spontaneous. They reflect a routine, an attitude, a quality of life. They are founded upon God's gifts of the Spirit.

Each of us must wonder, "Would I have been the one to return to give thanks?"

Perhaps we can never know for sure. But there is one thing we can do. Each and every day we can raise this prayer: Of all the things we ask this day, Lord, give to us the gift of a grateful heart.[5]

After such a prayer, reguarly prayed, our first question will answer itself. Thanksgiving is, after all, a spontaneous routine.

Oh yes! There is one thing more: Those who do return to give thanks, those who respond with hearts of gratitude to God for his blessings, open themselves for God to do still more. "And he said to him. 'Rise and go your way; your faith has made you well.' " One clearly has the impression that Luke meant more than being healed from the dreaded disease. He already had that, and there seems no implication that the healing was revoked for the other nine. There is an extraordinary "something more" here. What must it be like to be well, fully well, in God's eyes, to be "shalom?"

Consider this: What would it be like to live in such a way that we could be spontaneously grateful, routinely joyful, and at peace?

---

1. George H. Bush, "The President's Thanksgiving Proclamation of November 14, 1990." The quotation of President Washington is as it is quoted in the 1990 Proclamation.

2. Karl Menninger, M.D., *Whatever Became of Sin?*, (New York, Hawthorn Books, Inc., Publishers, 1973), p. 14.

3. John Baillie, *A Diary of Readings*, (New York, Charles Scribner's Sons, 1955), "Day 45," quoting Dr. Albert Schweitzer. One cannot be sure from the excerpt of Dr. Schweitzer's writing whether the "refreshed soul" is that of the healer or the healed. Luke will suggest the latter.

4. Martin Luther, "The Small Catechism," *The Book of Concord,* Theodore G. Tappert, Translator and Editor, (Philadelphia, Fortress Press, 1959), p. 345.

5. "Gratefulness," *The Works of George Herbert,* F. E. Hutchinson, Editor, (Oxford, Claredon Press, 1941), p. 123.

Lectionary Preaching After Pentecost

Virtually all pastors who make use of the sermons in this book will find their worship life and planning shaped by one of two lectionary series. Most mainline Protestant denominations, along with clergy of the Roman Catholic Church, have now approved — either for provisional or official use — the three-year Common (Consensus) Lectionary. This family of denominations includes United Methodist, Presbyterian, United Church of Christ and Disciples of Christ.

Lutherans and Roman Catholics, while testing the Common Lectionary on a limited basis at present, follow their own three-year cycle of texts. While there are divergences between the Common and Lutheran/Roman Catholic systems, the gospel texts show striking parallels, with few text selections evidencing significant differences. Nearly all the gospel texts included in this book will, therefore, be applicable to worship and preaching planning for clergy following either lectionary.

A significant divergence does occur, however, in the method by which specific gospel texts are assigned to specific calendar days. The Common and Roman Catholic Lectionaries accomplish this by counting backwards from Christ the King (Last Sunday after Pentecost), discarding "extra" texts from the front of the list: Lutherans follow the opposite pattern, counting forward from The Holy Trinity, discarding "extra" texts at the end of the list.

The following index will aid the user of this book in matching the correct text to the correct Sunday during the Pentecost portion of the church year.

(Fixed dates do not pertain to Lutheran Lectionary)

Fixed Date Lectionaries *Common and Roman Catholic*	Lutheran Lectionary *Lutheran*
The Day of Pentecost	The Day of Pentecost
The Holy Trinity	The Holy Trinity
May 29-June 4 — Proper 4, Ordinary Time 9	Pentecost 2
June 5-11 — Proper 5, Ordinary Time 10	Pentecost 3
June 12-18 — Proper 6, Ordinary Time 11	Pentecost 4
June 19-25 — Proper 7, Ordinary Time 12	Pentecost 5
June 26-July 2 — Proper 8, Ordinary Time 13	Pentecost 6

July 3-9 — Proper 9, Ordinary Time 14	Pentecost 7
July 10-16 — Proper 10, Ordinary Time 15	Pentecost 8
July 17-23 — Proper 11, Ordinary Time 16	Pentecost 9
July 24-30 — Proper 12, Ordinary Time 17	Pentecost 10
July 31-Aug. 6 — Proper 13, Ordinary Time 18	Pentecost 11
Aug. 7-13 — Proper 14, Ordinary Time 19	Pentecost 12
Aug. 14-20 — Proper 15, Ordinary Time 20	Pentecost 13
Aug. 21-27 — Proper 16, Ordinary Time 21	Pentecost 14
Aug. 28-Sept. 3 — Proper 17, Ordinary Time 22	Pentecost 15
Sept. 4-10 — Proper 18, Ordinary Time 23	Pentecost 16
Sept. 11-17 — Proper 19, Ordinary Time 24	Pentecost 17
Sept. 18-24 — Proper 20, Ordinary Time 25	Pentecost 18
Sept. 25-Oct. 1 — Proper 21, Ordinary Time 26	Pentecost 19
Oct. 2-8 — Proper 22, Ordinary Time 27	Pentecost 20
Oct. 9-15 — Proper 23, Ordinary Time 28	Pentecost 21
Oct. 16-22 — Proper 24, Ordinary Time 29	Pentecost 22
Oct. 23-29 — Proper 25, Ordinary Time 30	Pentecost 23
Oct. 30-Nov. 5 — Proper 26, Ordinary Time 31	Pentecost 24
Nov. 6-12 — Proper 27, Ordinary Time 32	Pentecost 25
Nov. 13-19 — Proper 28, Ordinary Time 33	Pentecost 26 Pentecost 27
Nov. 20-26 — Christ the King	Christ the King

Reformation Day (or last Sunday in October) is October 31 (Common, Lutheran)

All Saints' Day (or first Sunday in November) is November 1 (Common, Lutheran, Roman Catholic)

135